Aggretsuko™

METAL TO THE MAX

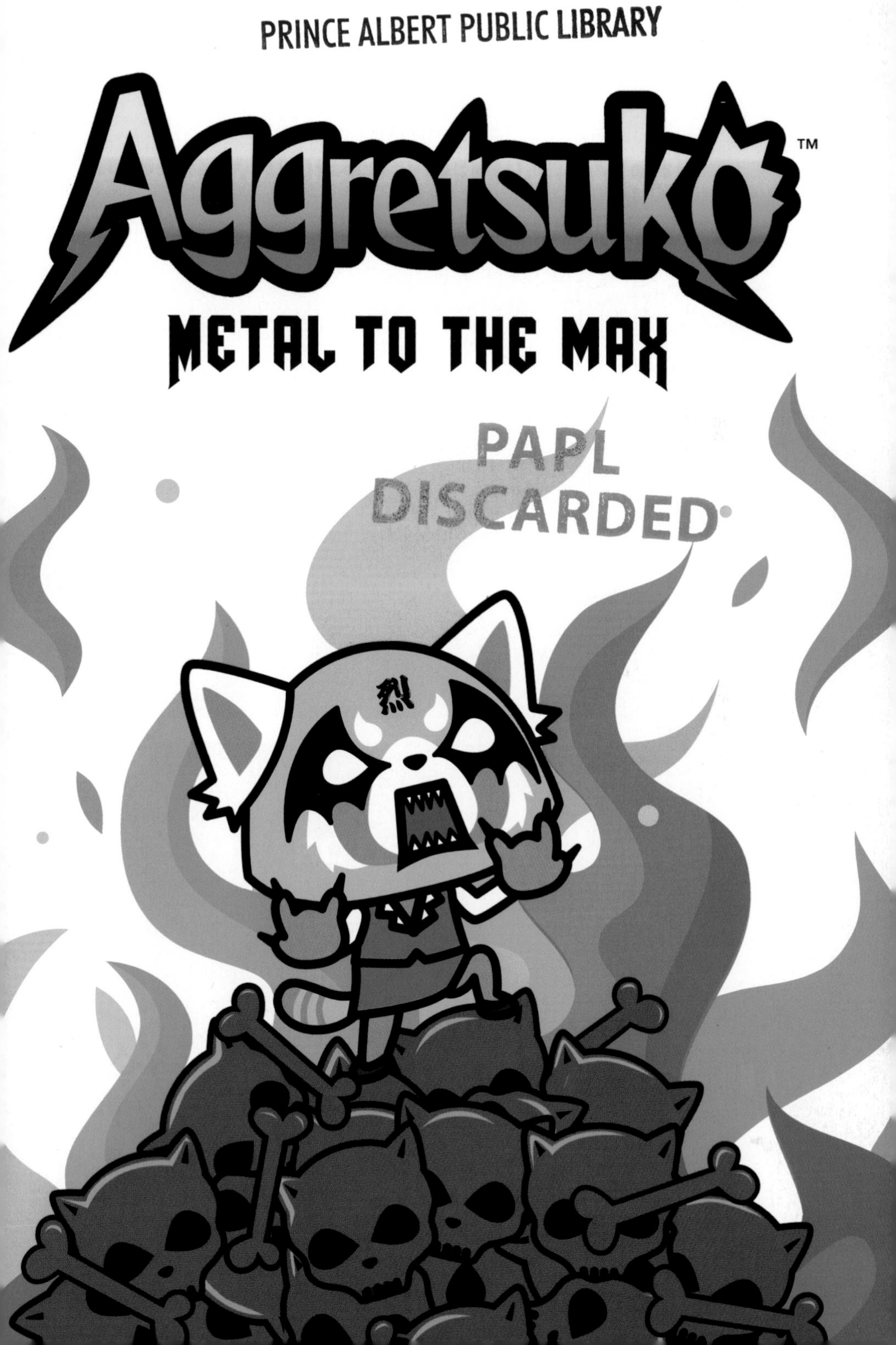

DOWN WITH THE SICKNESS

WRITTEN BY Daniel Barnes ILLUSTRATED BY D.J. Kirkland

MALL MADNESS

WRITTEN AND ILLUSTRATED BY Jarrett Williams

THE VISITOR

WRITTEN AND ILLUSTRATED BY Brenda Hickey

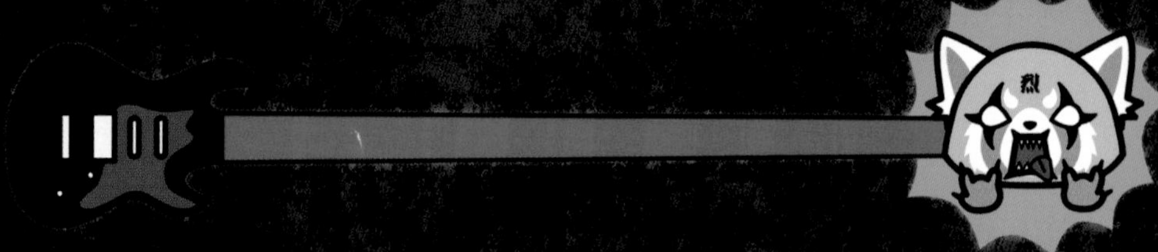

ALL PAGES COLORED BY Sarah Stern ALL PAGES LETTERED BY Crank!

REGULAR COVER BY C.J. Cannon VARIANT COVER BY D.J. Kirkland

Aggretsuko™

METAL TO THE MAX

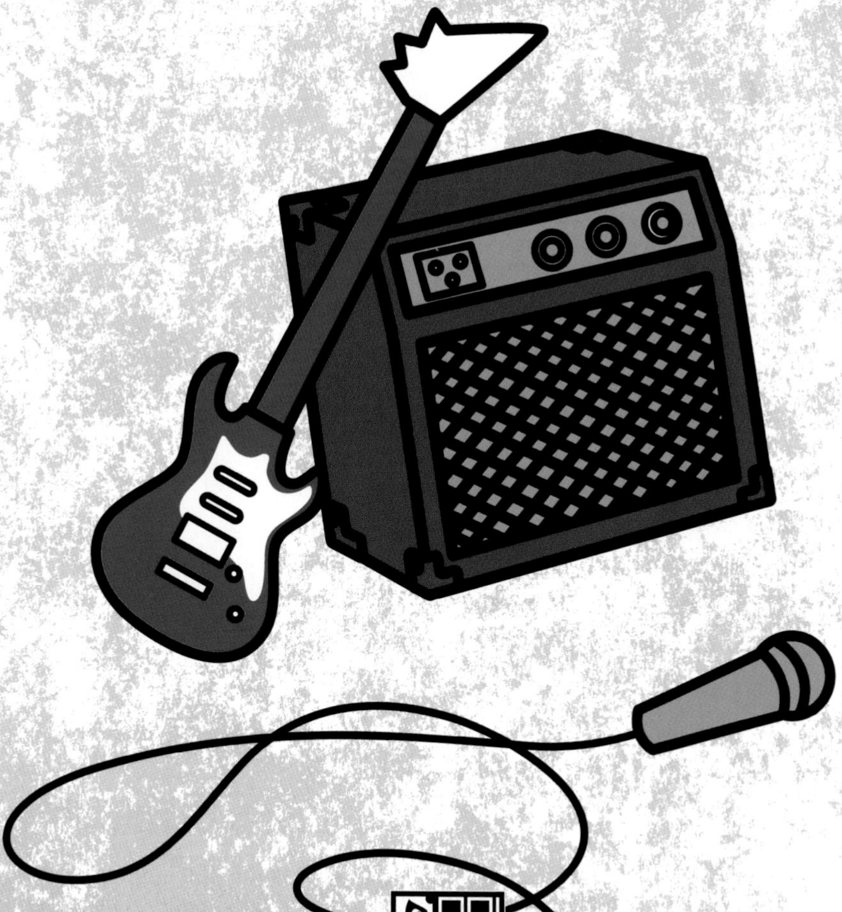

AN ONI PRESS PUBLICATION

DESIGNED BY SARAH ROCKWELL   **EDITED BY** SARAH GAYDOS

SPECIAL THANKS TO
CINDY SUZUKI, JEFF PARKER, MARJORIE SANTOS,
SUZAN ZHANG, SUSAN TRAN, RENEE HAMMER,
ELLEN IZYKOWSKI, AND LINH FORSE

onipress.com

@onipress

lionforge.com

@lionforge

sanrio.com

@sanrio

@aggretsuko

aggretsuko

@aggretsuko

aggretsuko

Aggretsuko™
by Sanrio®
©2015, 2020 SANRIO CO., LTD.
S/T·F
Used Under License.
www.sanrio.com

SIL-34865

PUBLISHED BY ONI-LION FORGE PUBLISHING GROUP, LLC
James Lucas Jones, president & publisher
Sarah Gaydos, editor in chief **Charlie Chu**, e.v.p.
of creative & business development **Brad Rooks**,
director of operations **Amber O'Neill**, special
projects manager **Harris Fish**, events manager
Margot Wood, director of marketing & sales **J
Devin Funches**, sales & marketing manager
Katie Sainz, marketing manager **Tara Lehmann**,
marketing & publicity associate **Troy Look**,
director of design & production **Kate Z. Stone**,
senior graphic designer **Sonja Synak**, graphic
designer **Hilary Thompson**, graphic designer
Sarah Rockwell, junior graphic designer **Angie
Knowles**, digital prepress lead **Vincent Kukua**,
digital prepress technician **Jasmine Amiri**, senior
editor **Shawna Gore**, senior editor **Amanda
Meadows**, senior editor **Robert Meyers**, senior
editor, licensing **Grace Bornhoft**, editor **Zack
Soto**, editor **Chris Cerasi**, editorial coordinator
Steve Ellis, vice president of games **Ben Eisner**,
game developer **Michelle Nguyen**, executive
assistant **Jung Lee**, logistics coordinator
Joe Nozemack, publisher emeritus

First Edition: August 2020
REGULAR ISBN 978-1-62010-718-8
ONI EXCLUSIVE VARIANT ISBN 978-1-62010-772-0
eISBN 978-1-62010-725-6

Printing numbers:
1 2 3 4 5 6 7 8 9 10

Library of Congress Control Number 2020934133

Printed in South Korea through
Four Colour Print Group, Louisville, KY.

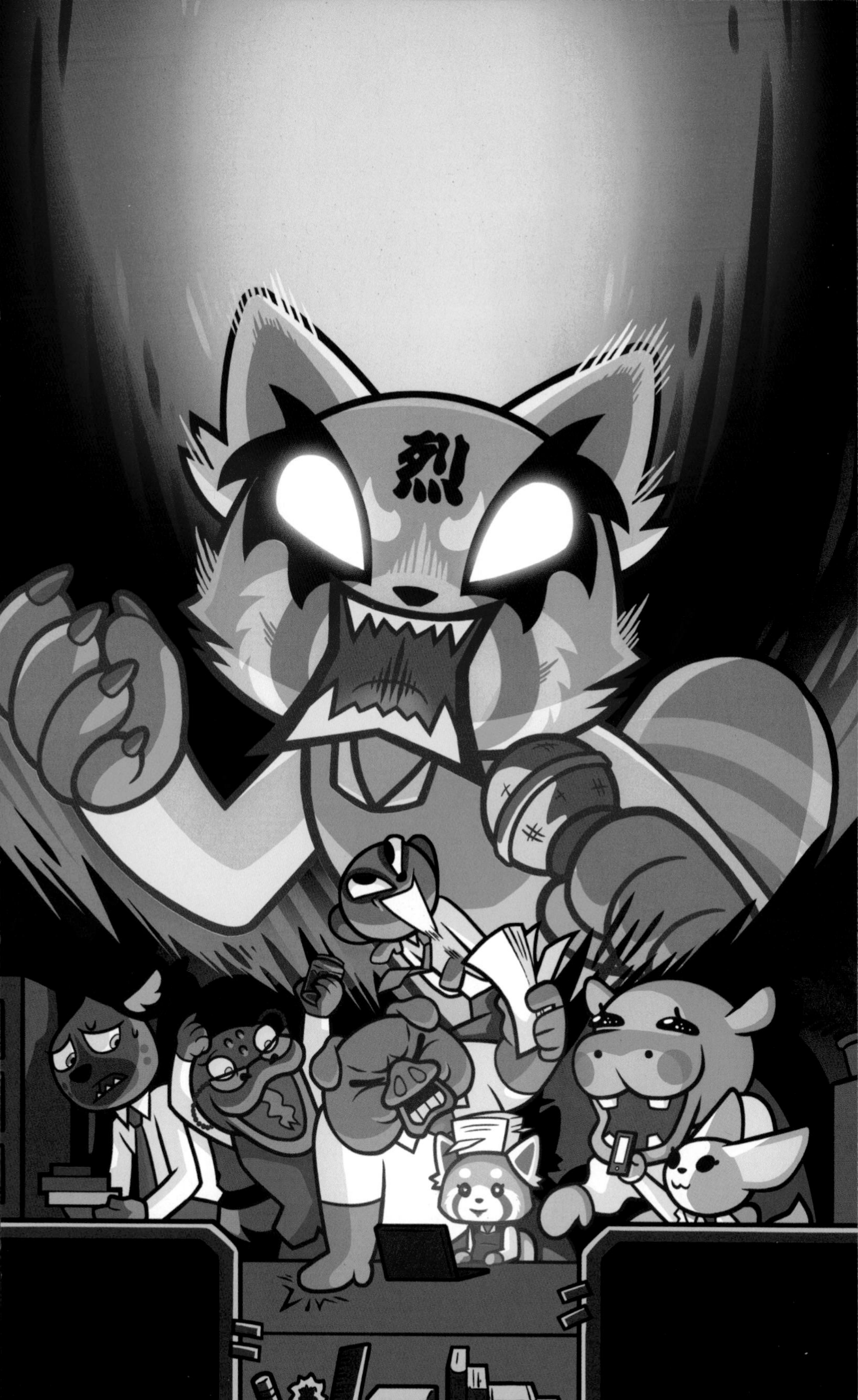
烈

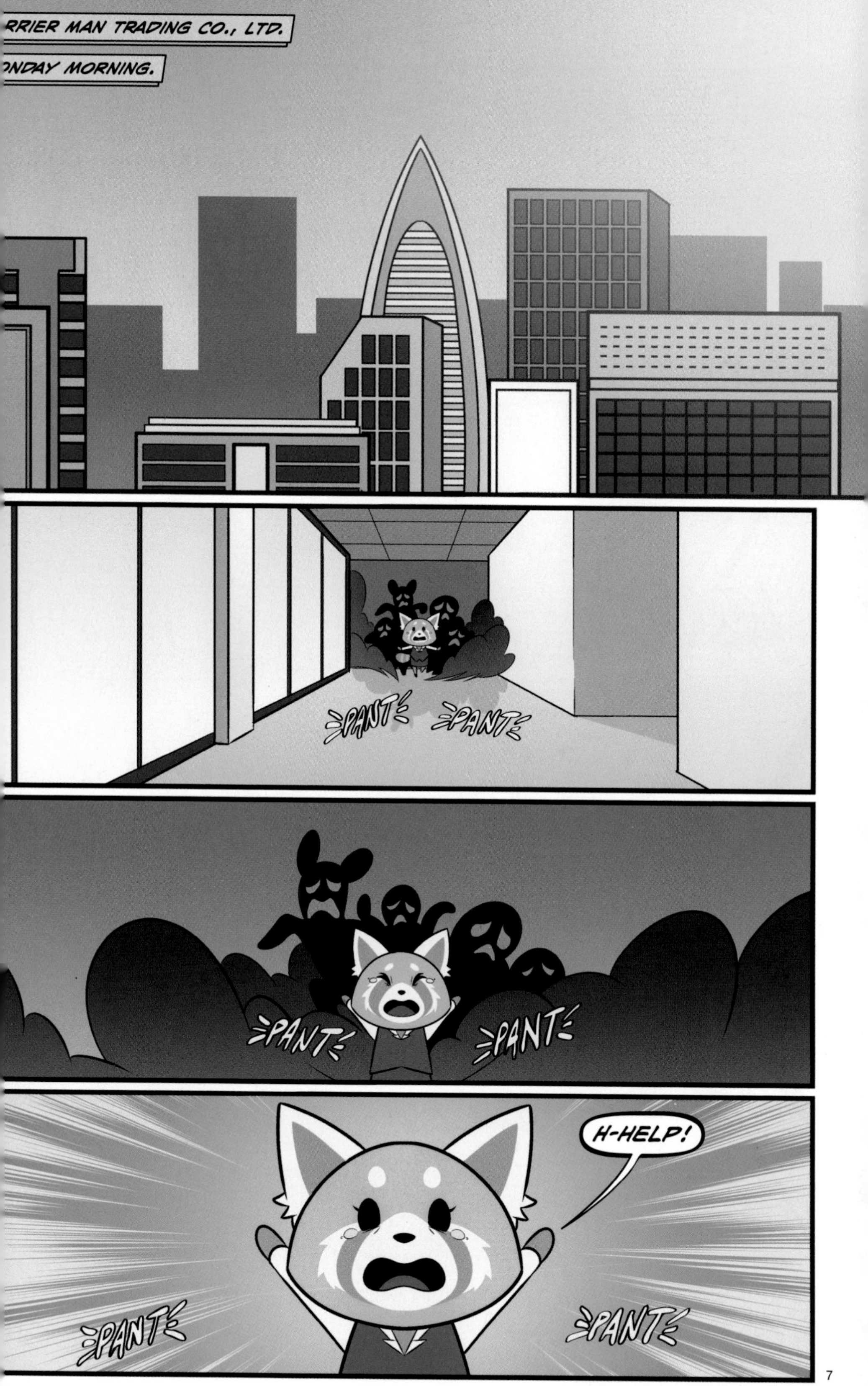
RRIER MAN TRADING CO., LTD.
ONDAY MORNING.
PANT PANT
PANT PANT
H-HELP!
PANT PANT

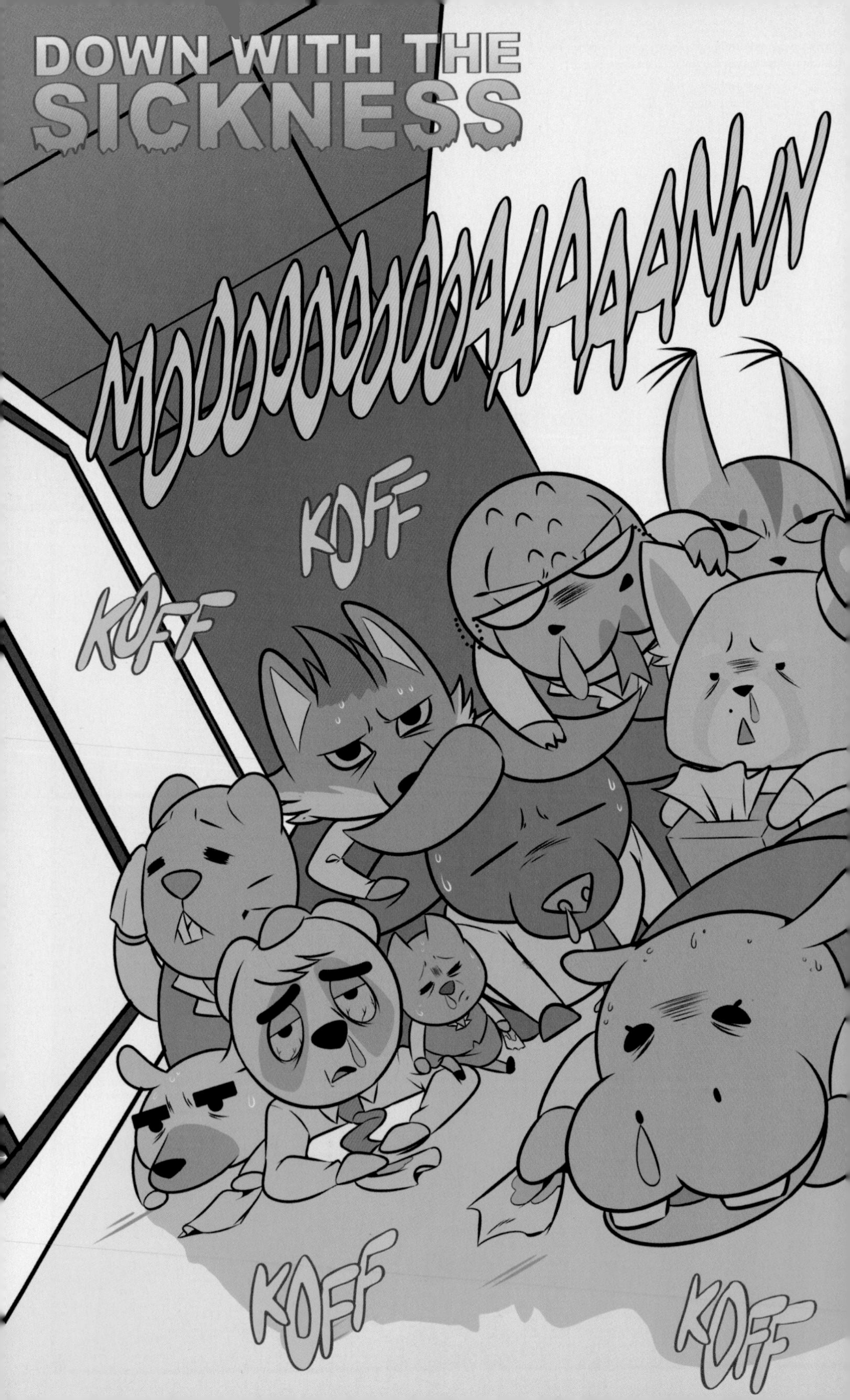
DOWN WITH THE SICKNESS
MOOOOOOOOAAAAAANNN
KOFF
KOFF
KOFF
KOFF

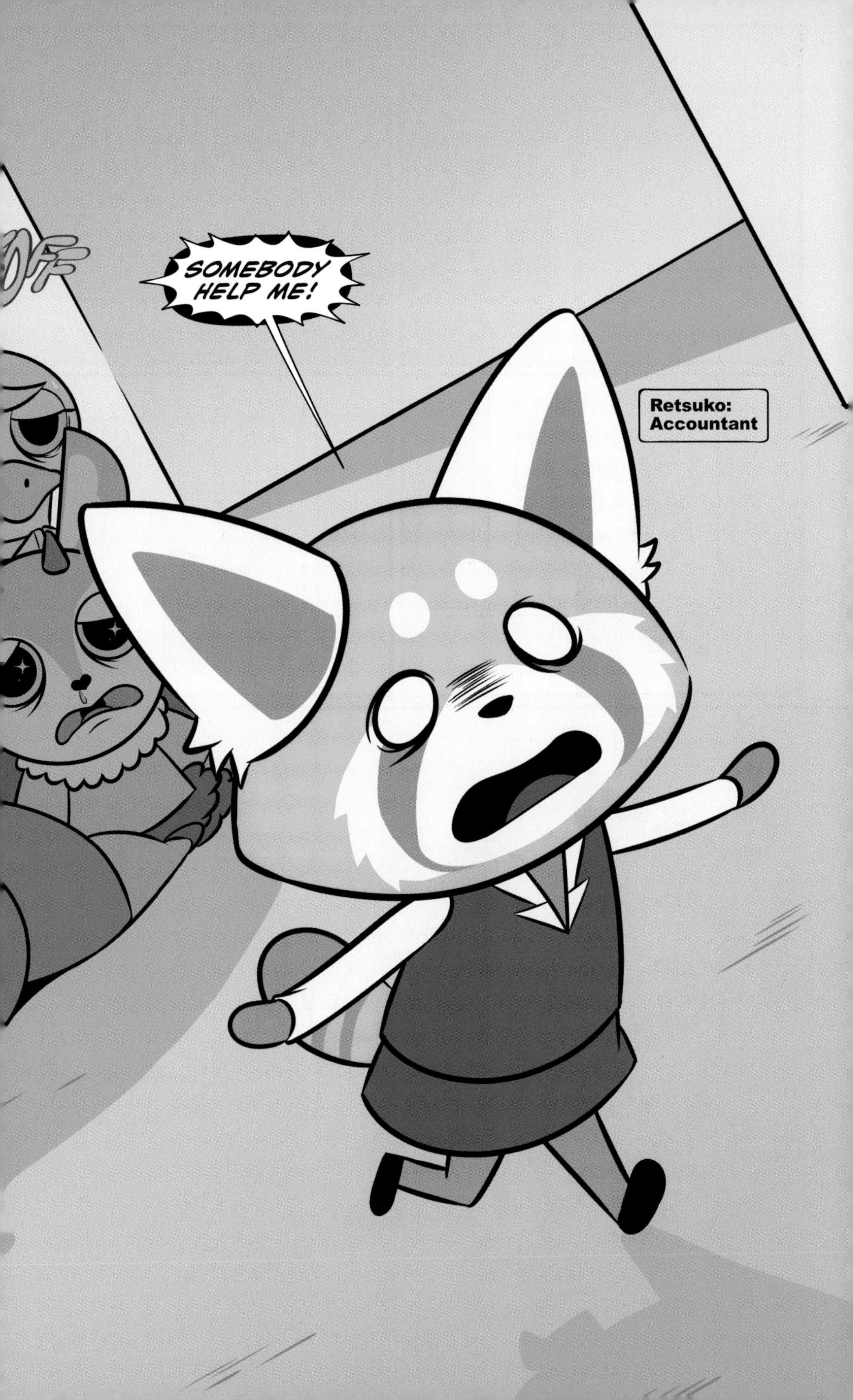
OFF
SOMEBODY HELP ME!
Retsuko: Accountant

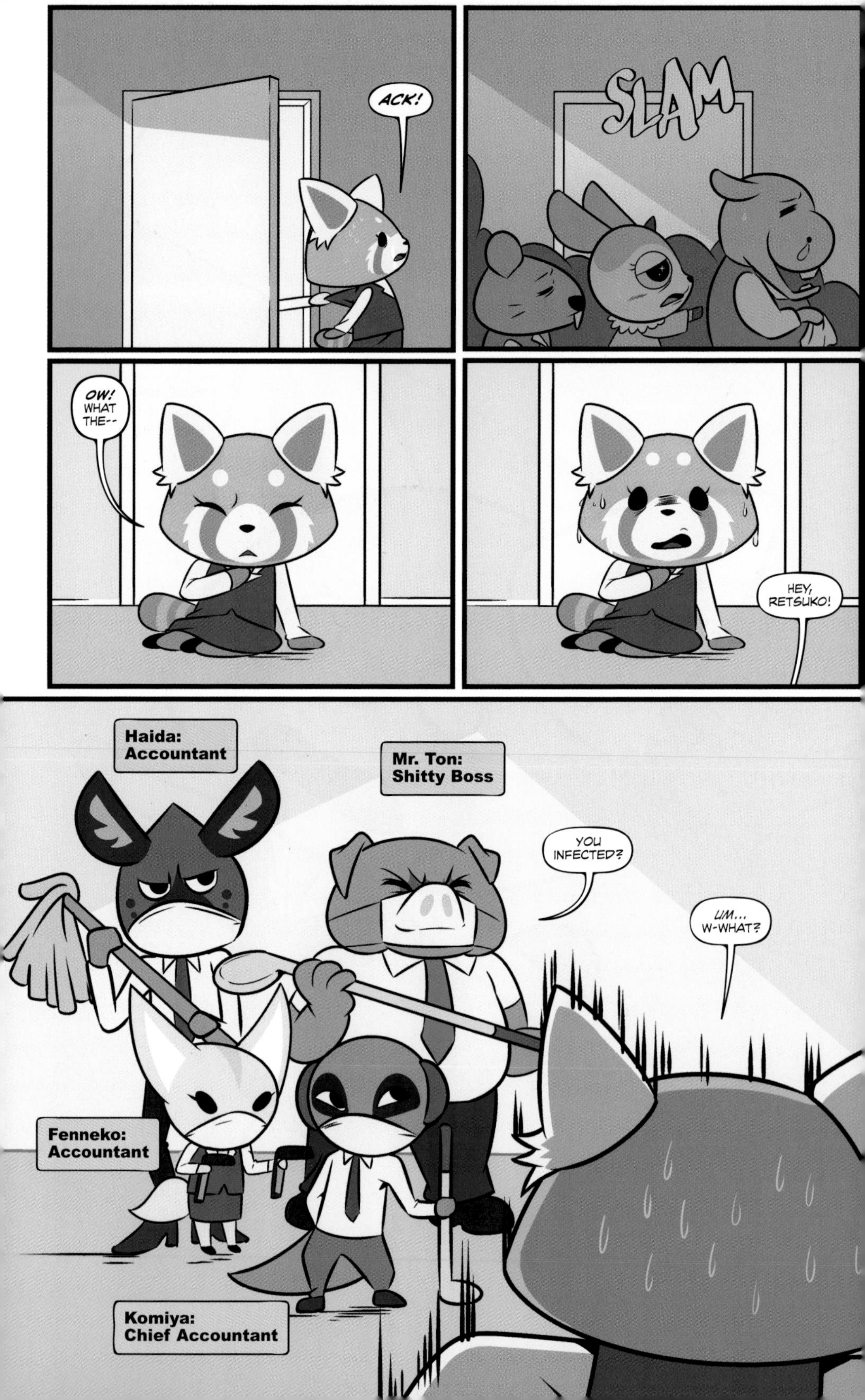
ACK!
SLAM
OW! WHAT THE--
HEY, RETSUKO!
Haida: Accountant
Mr. Ton: Shitty Boss
YOU INFECTED?
UM... W-WHAT?
Fenneko: Accountant
Komiya: Chief Accountant

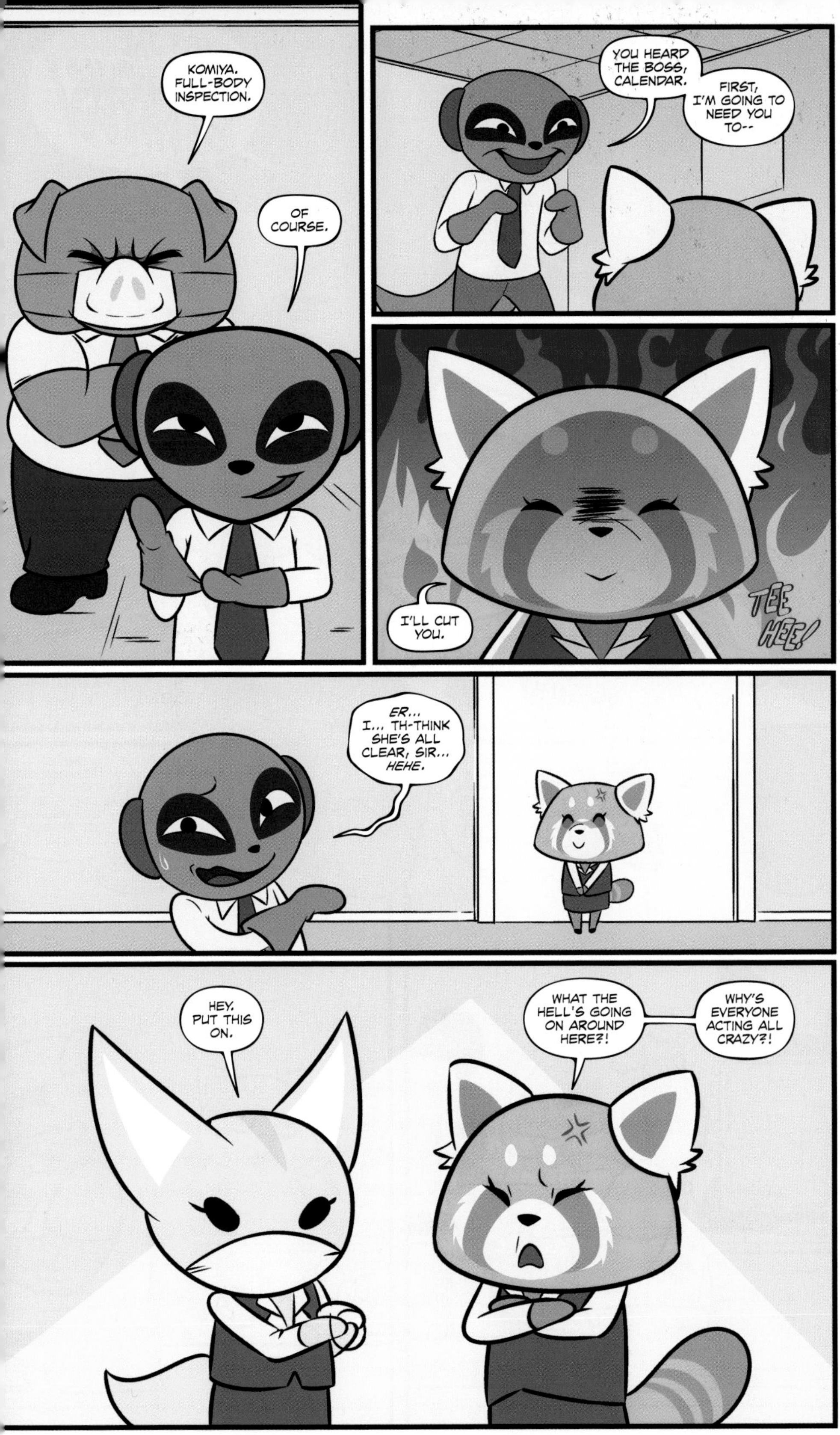
KOMIYA. FULL-BODY INSPECTION.
OF COURSE.
YOU HEARD THE BOSS, CALENDAR.
FIRST, I'M GOING TO NEED YOU TO--
I'LL CUT YOU.
TEE HEE!
ER... I... TH-THINK SHE'S ALL CLEAR, SIR... HEHE.
HEY. PUT THIS ON.
WHAT THE HELL'S GOING ON AROUND HERE?!
WHY'S EVERYONE ACTING ALL CRAZY?!

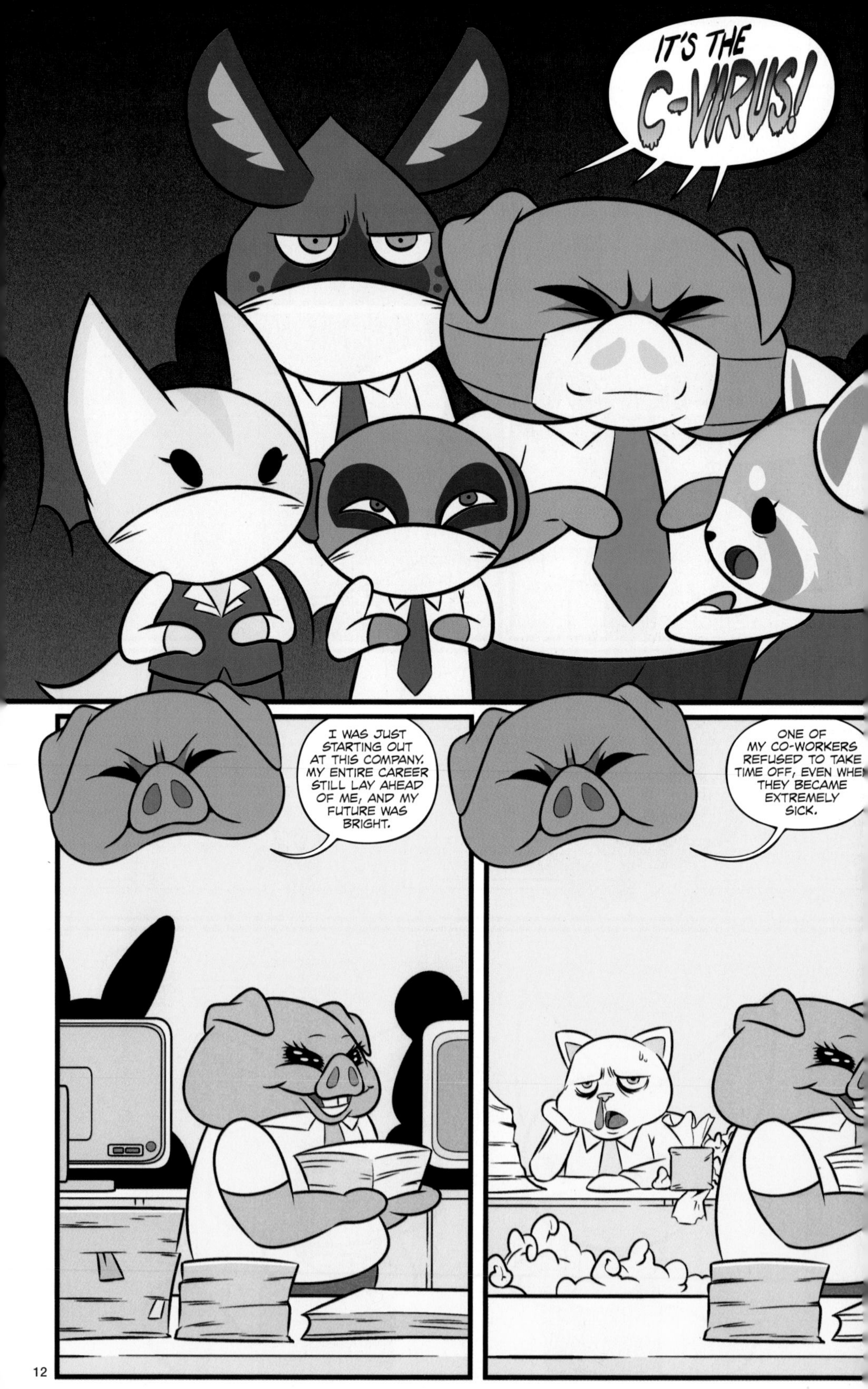
IT'S THE C-VIRUS!
I WAS JUST STARTING OUT AT THIS COMPANY. MY ENTIRE CAREER STILL LAY AHEAD OF ME, AND MY FUTURE WAS BRIGHT.
ONE OF MY CO-WORKERS REFUSED TO TAKE TIME OFF, EVEN WHE THEY BECAME EXTREMELY SICK.

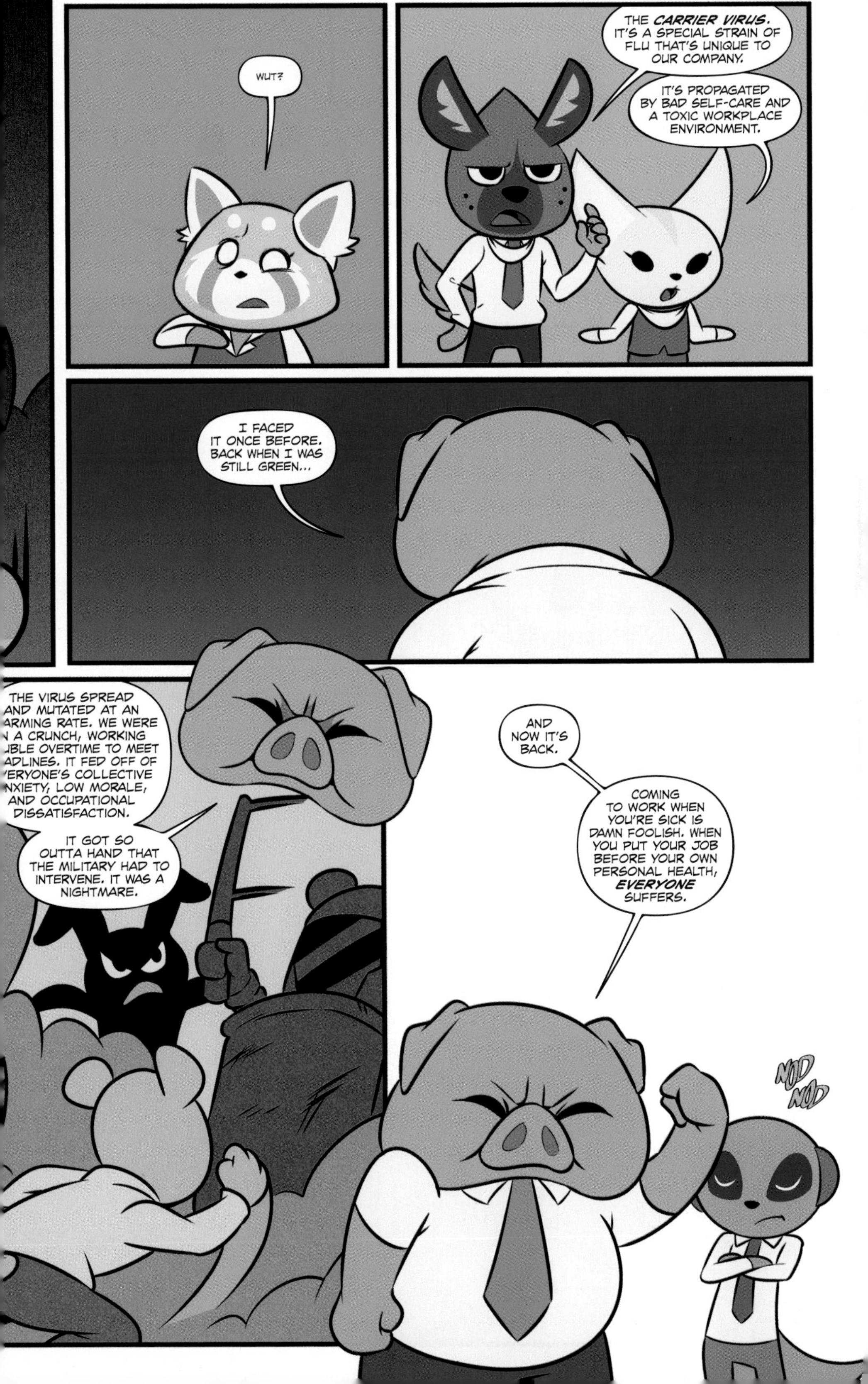
WUT?
THE CARRIER VIRUS. IT'S A SPECIAL STRAIN OF FLU THAT'S UNIQUE TO OUR COMPANY.
IT'S PROPAGATED BY BAD SELF-CARE AND A TOXIC WORKPLACE ENVIRONMENT.
I FACED IT ONCE BEFORE. BACK WHEN I WAS STILL GREEN...
THE VIRUS SPREAD AND MUTATED AT AN ARMING RATE. WE WERE N A CRUNCH, WORKING UBLE OVERTIME TO MEET ADLINES. IT FED OFF OF VERYONE'S COLLECTIVE NXIETY, LOW MORALE, AND OCCUPATIONAL DISSATISFACTION.
IT GOT SO OUTTA HAND THAT THE MILITARY HAD TO INTERVENE. IT WAS A NIGHTMARE.
AND NOW IT'S BACK.
COMING TO WORK WHEN YOU'RE SICK IS DAMN FOOLISH. WHEN YOU PUT YOUR JOB BEFORE YOUR OWN PERSONAL HEALTH, EVERYONE SUFFERS.
NOD NOD

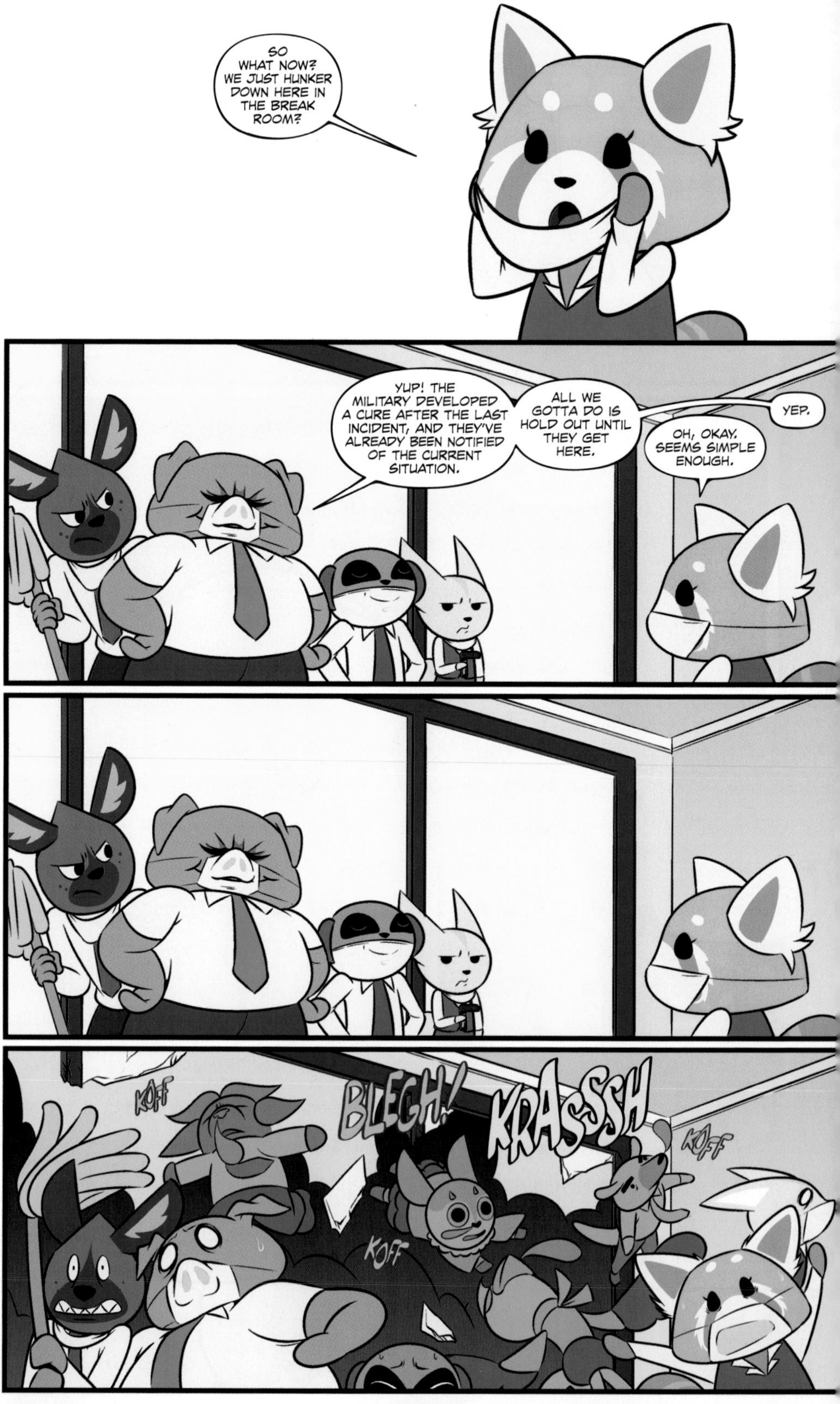
SO WHAT NOW? WE JUST HUNKER DOWN HERE IN THE BREAK ROOM?
YUP! THE MILITARY DEVELOPED A CURE AFTER THE LAST INCIDENT, AND THEY'VE ALREADY BEEN NOTIFIED OF THE CURRENT SITUATION.
ALL WE GOTTA DO IS HOLD OUT UNTIL THEY GET HERE.
YEP.
OH, OKAY. SEEMS SIMPLE ENOUGH.
KOFF
BLEGH!
KRASSSH
KOFF
KOFF

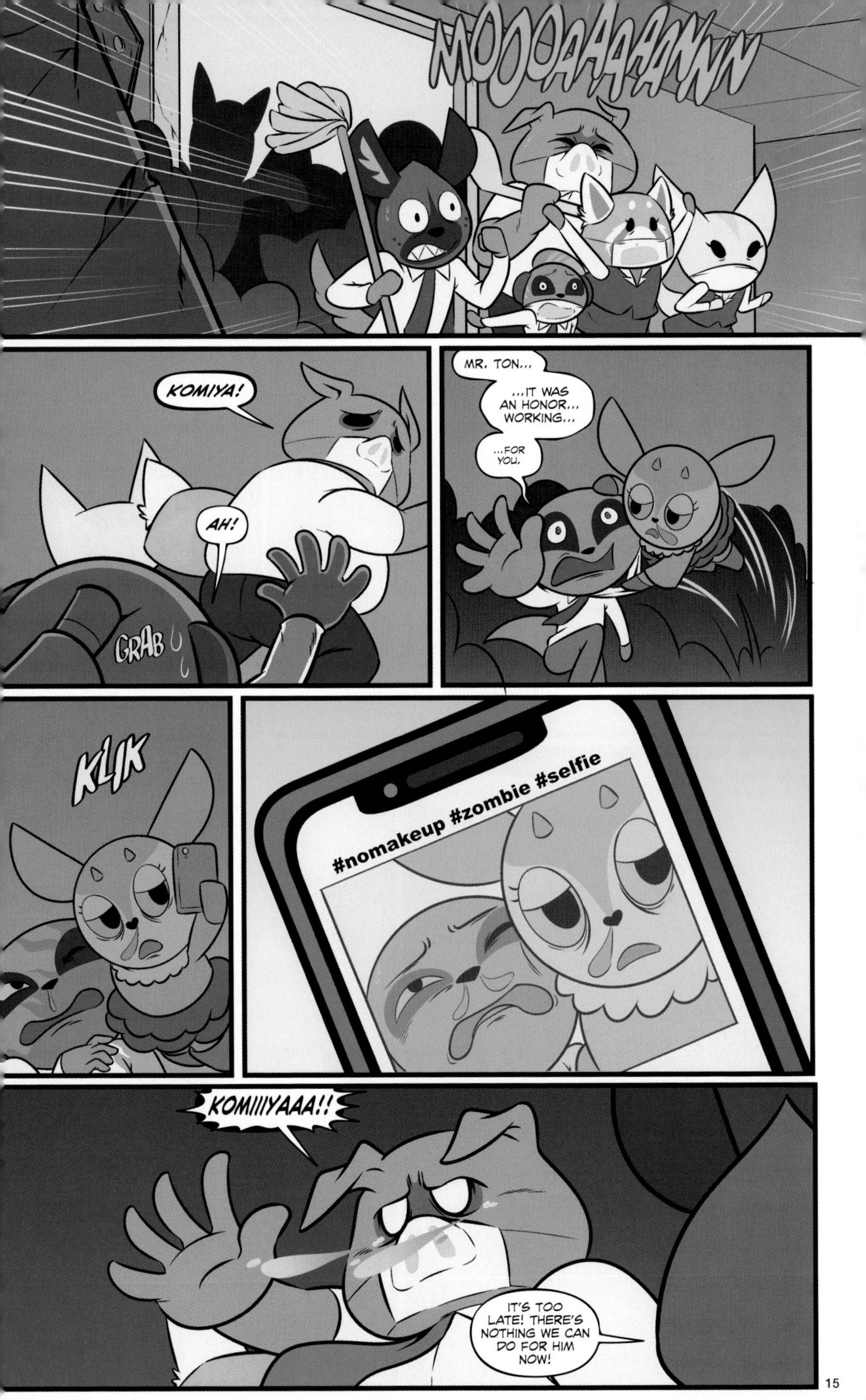
MOOOAAAANNN
KOMIYA!
AH!
GRAB
MR. TON...
...IT WAS AN HONOR... WORKING...
...FOR YOU.
KLIK
#nomakeup #zombie #selfie
KOMIIIYAAA!!
IT'S TOO LATE! THERE'S NOTHING WE CAN DO FOR HIM NOW!

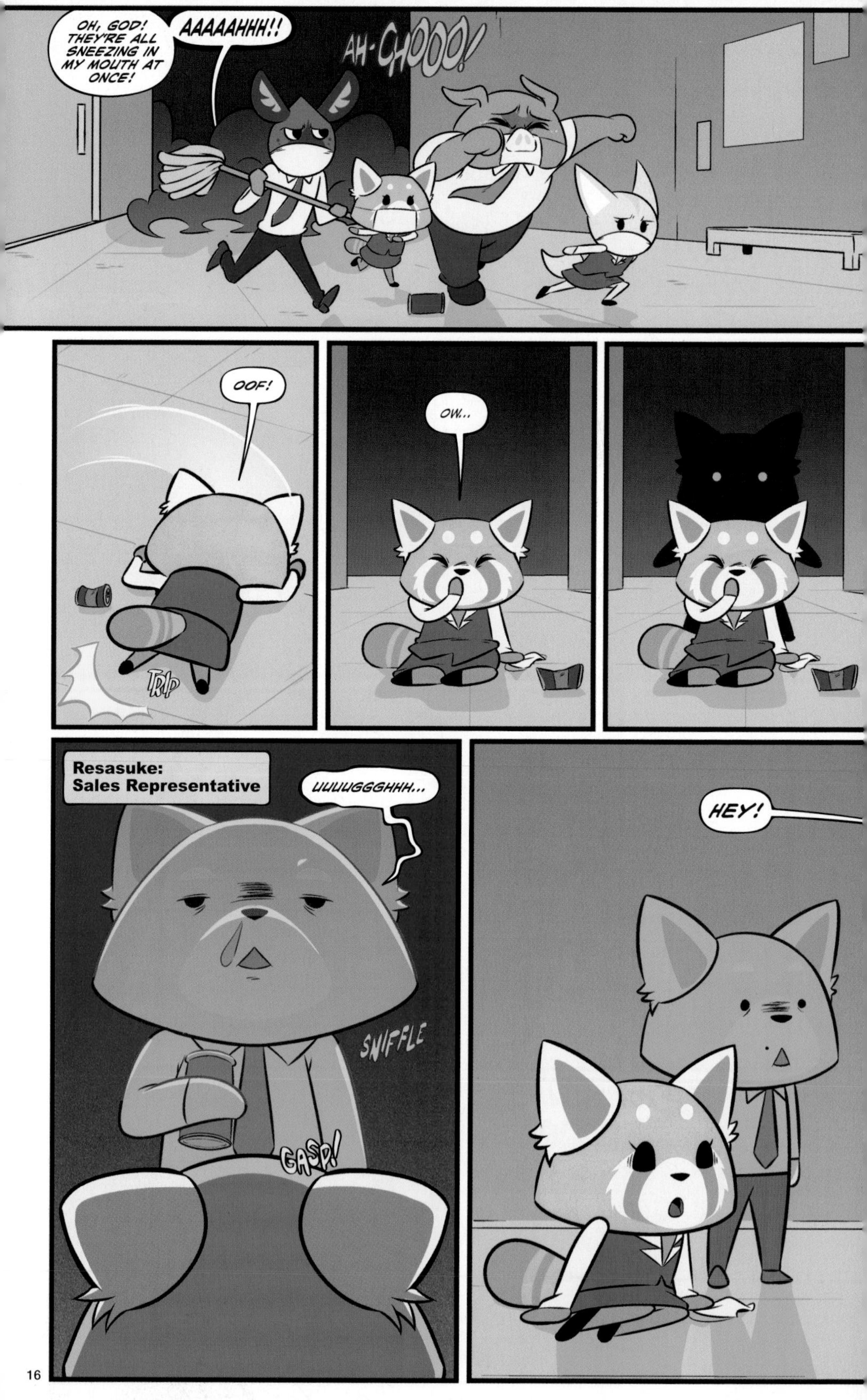
OH, GOD! THEY'RE ALL SNEEZING IN MY MOUTH AT ONCE!
AAAAAHHH!!
AH-CHOOO!
OOF!
TRIP
OW...
Resasuke: Sales Representative
UUUUGGGHHH...
SNIFFLE
GASP!
HEY!

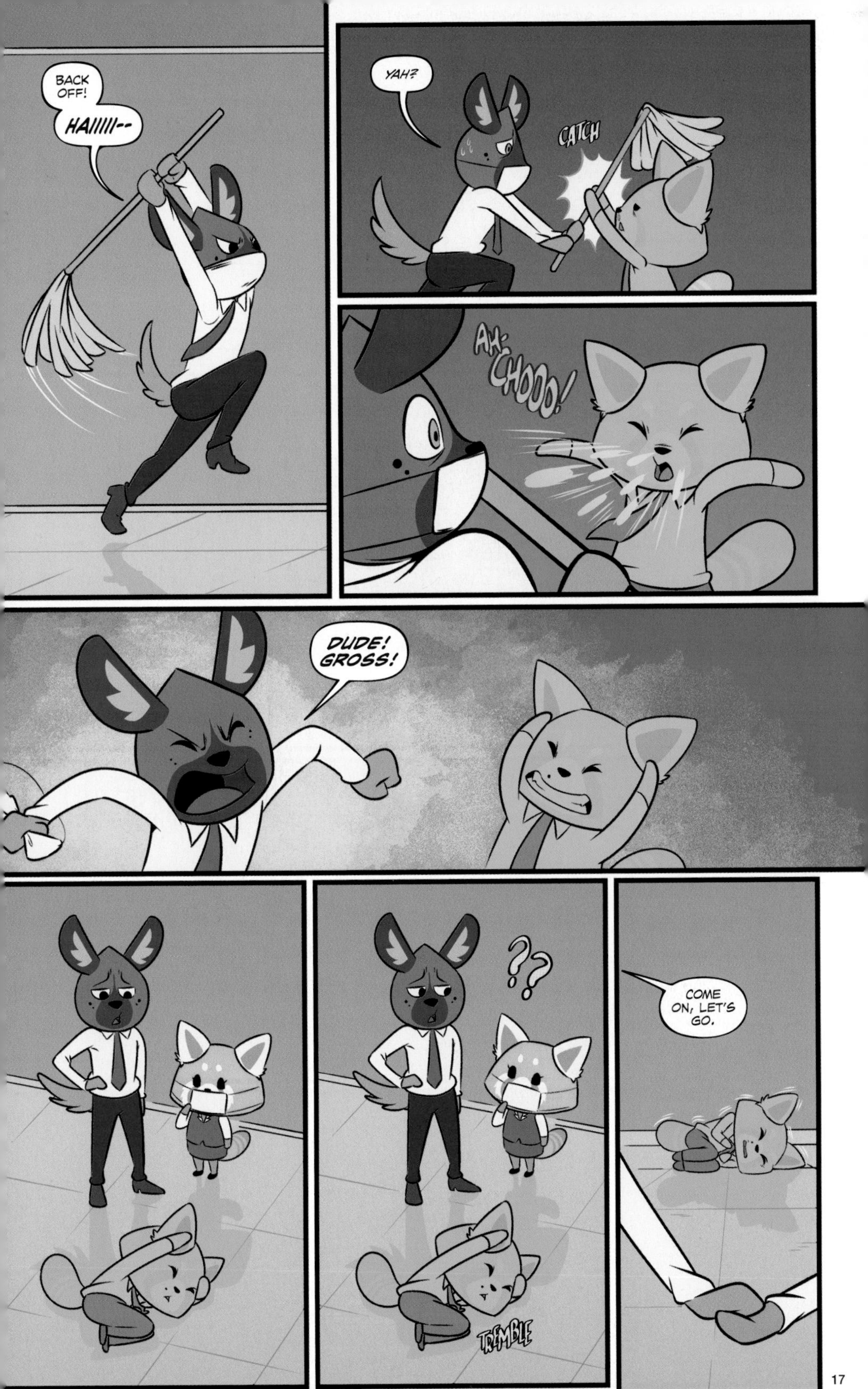
BACK OFF!
HAIIIII--
YAH?
CATCH
AH-CHOOO!
DUDE! GROSS!
??
TREMBLE
COME ON, LET'S GO.

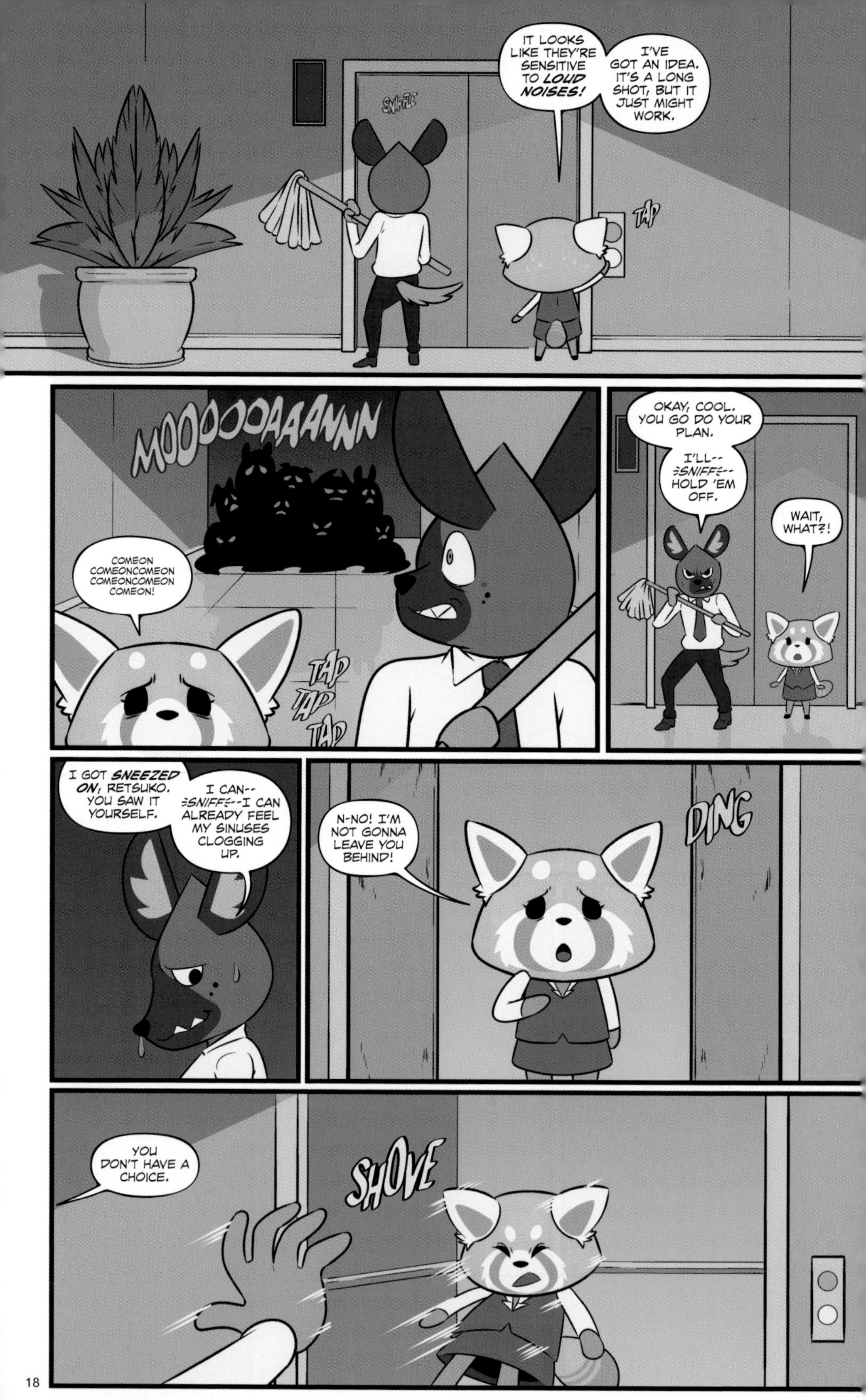
SNIFFLE
IT LOOKS LIKE THEY'RE SENSITIVE TO LOUD NOISES!
I'VE GOT AN IDEA. IT'S A LONG SHOT, BUT IT JUST MIGHT WORK.
TAP
MOOOOOAAAANNN
COMEON COMEONCOMEON COMEONCOMEON COMEON!
TAP TAP TAP
OKAY, COOL. YOU GO DO YOUR PLAN.
I'LL-- SNIFF-- HOLD 'EM OFF.
WAIT, WHAT?!
I GOT SNEEZED ON, RETSUKO. YOU SAW IT YOURSELF.
I CAN-- SNIFF--I CAN ALREADY FEEL MY SINUSES CLOGGING UP.
N-NO! I'M NOT GONNA LEAVE YOU BEHIND!
DING
YOU DON'T HAVE A CHOICE.
SHOVE

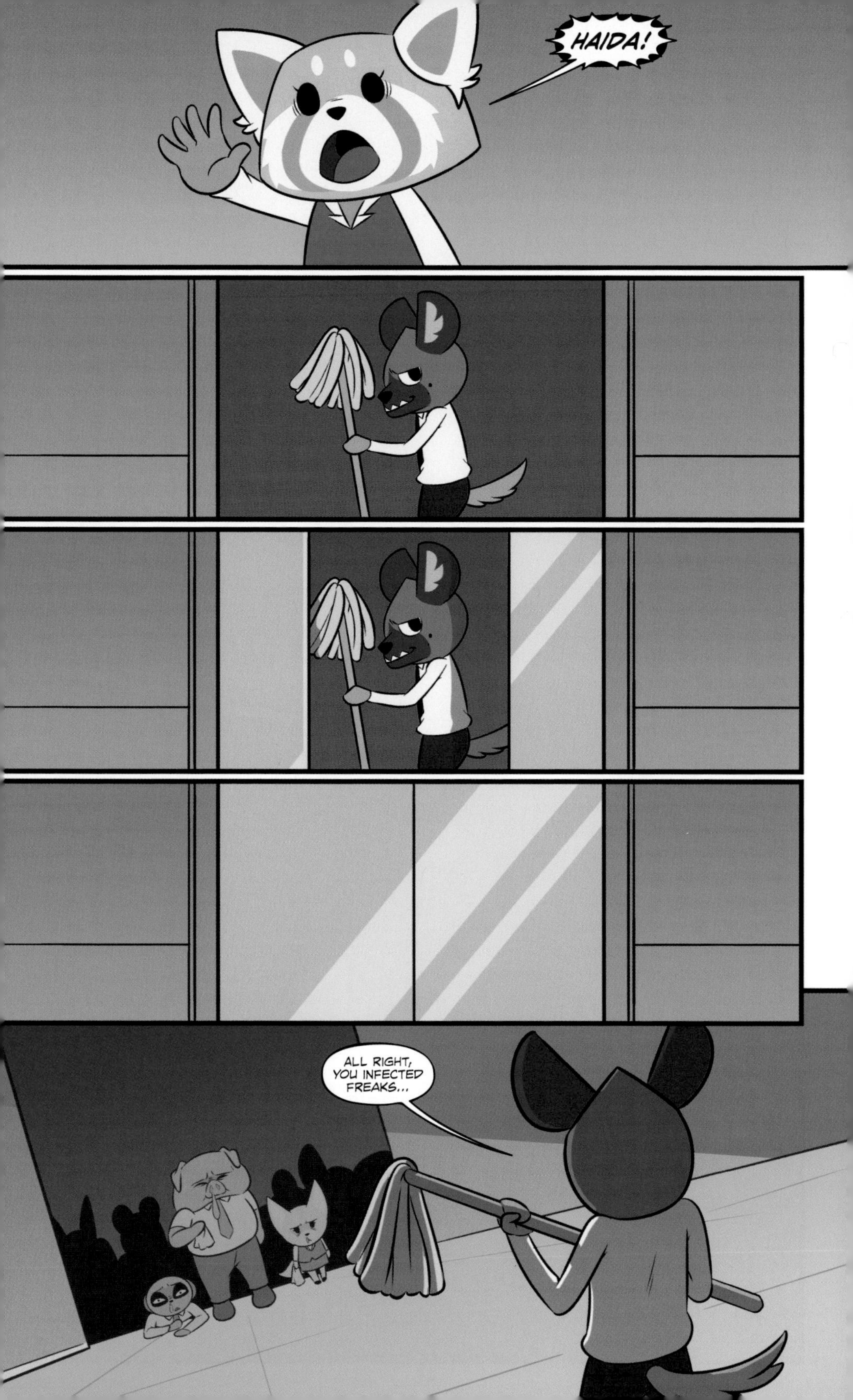
HAIDA!
ALL RIGHT, YOU INFECTED FREAKS...

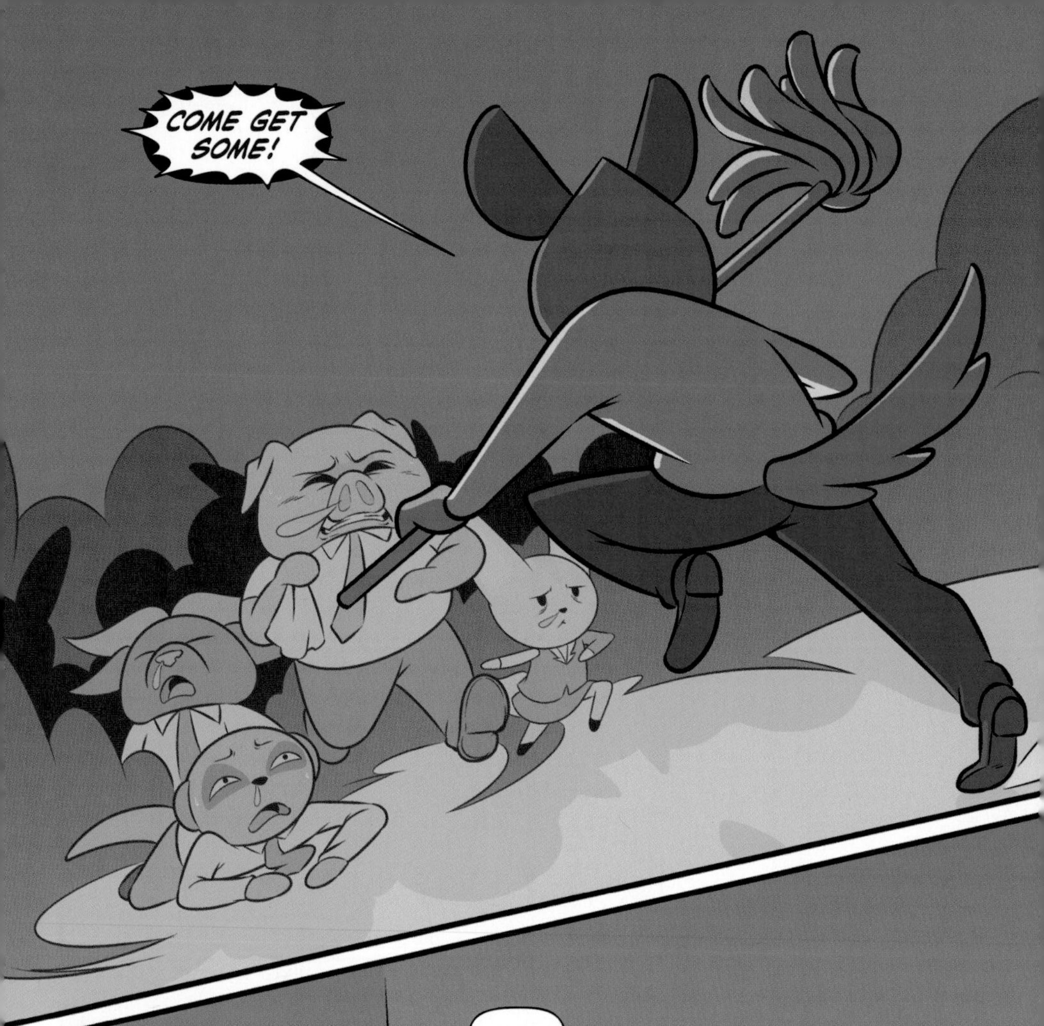
COME GET SOME!

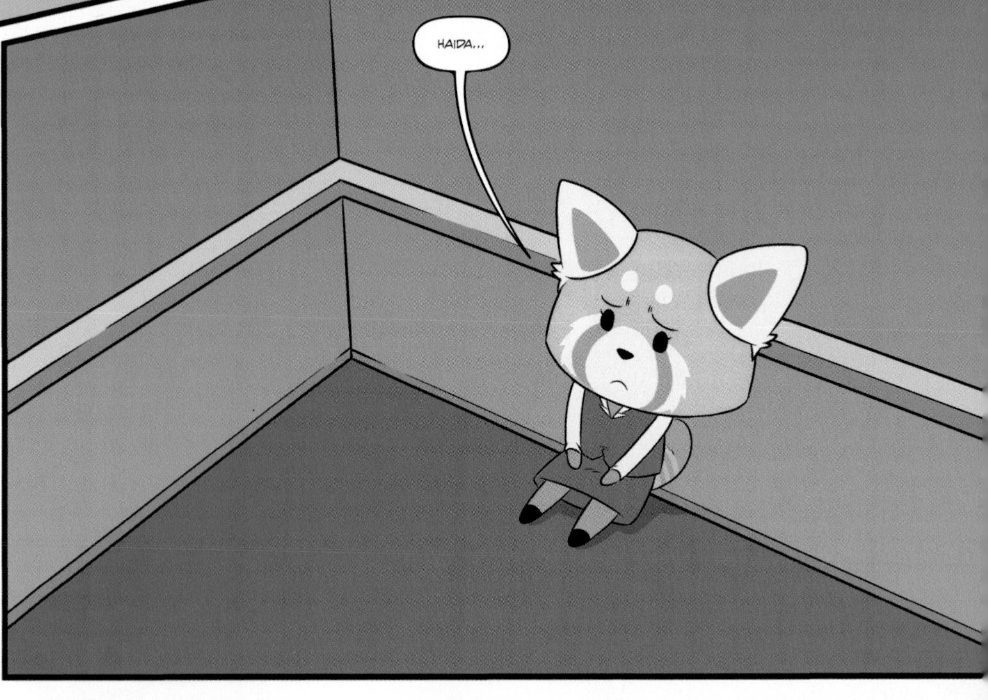
HAIDA...

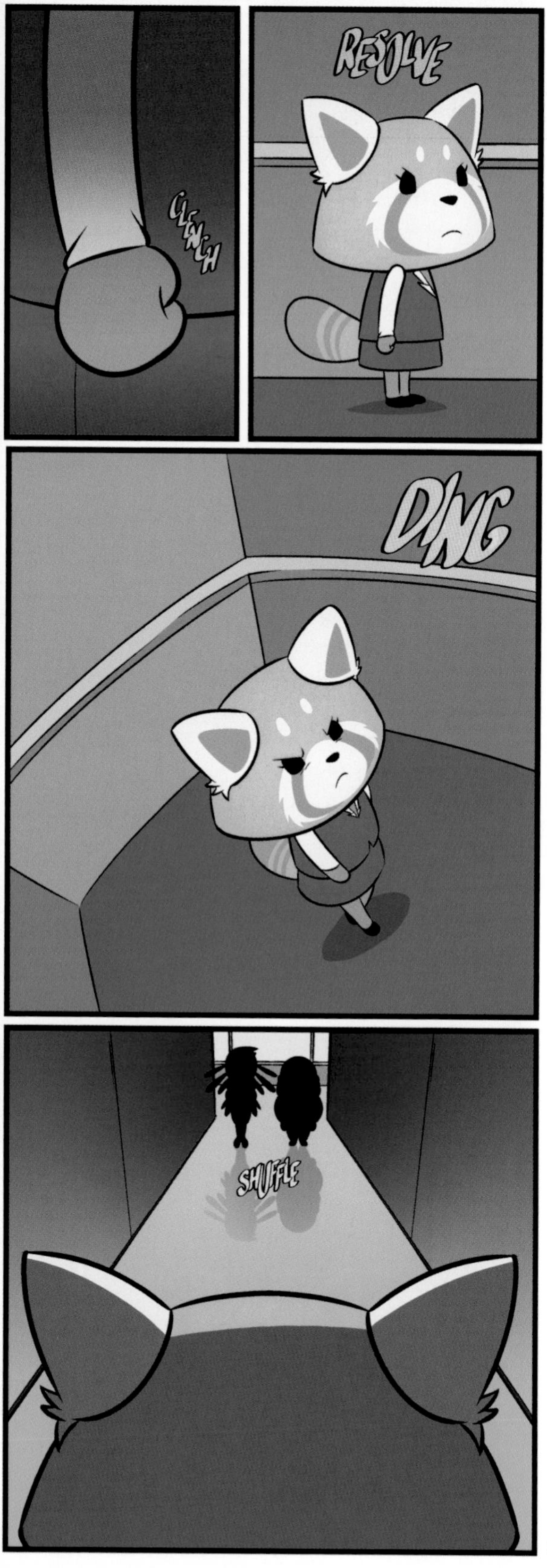
CLENCH
RESOLVE
DING
SHUFFLE

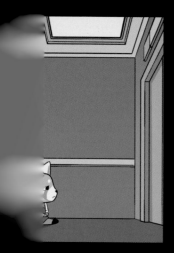

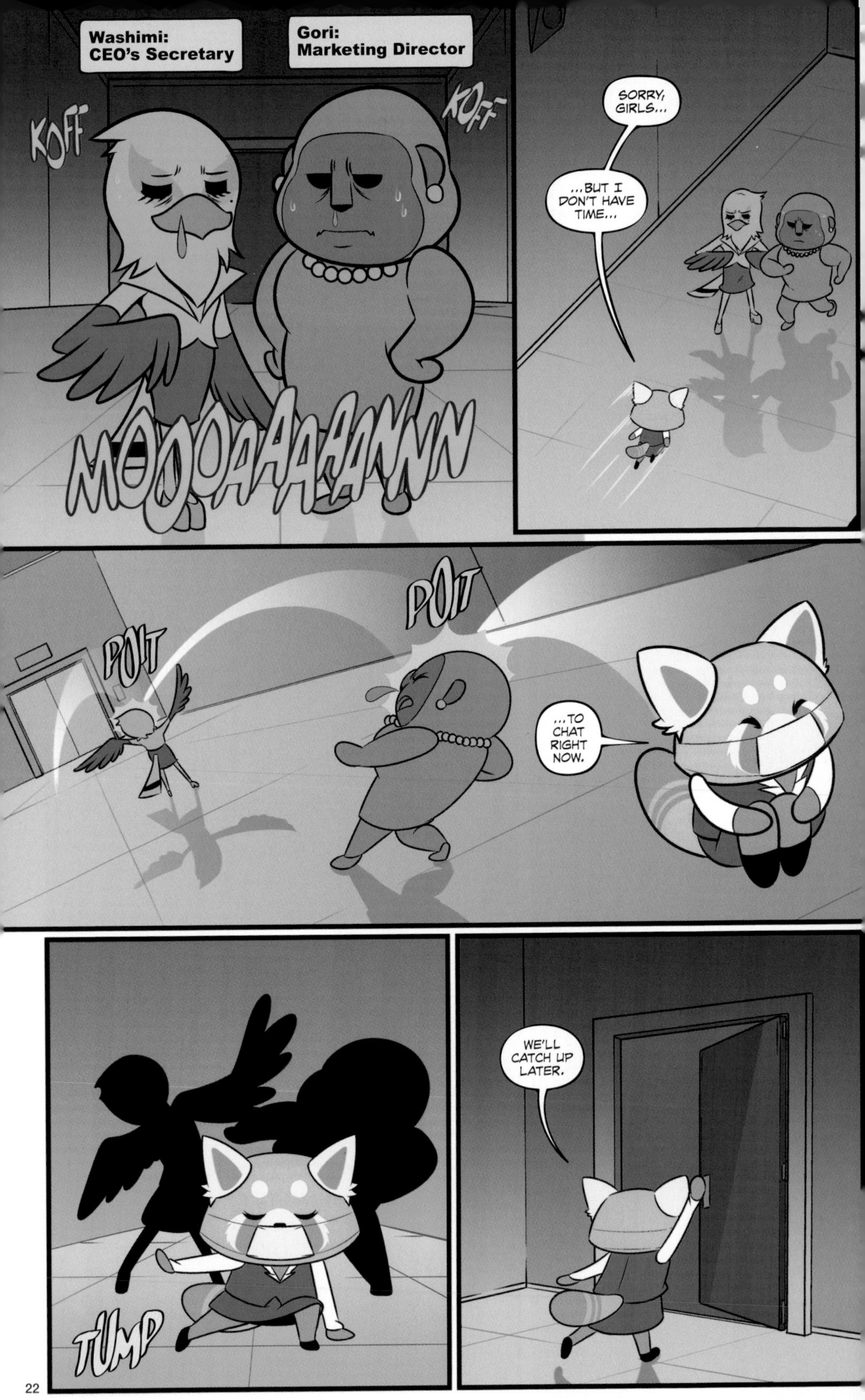
Washimi:
CEO's Secretary
Gori:
Marketing Director
KOFF
KOFF
MOOOAAAAANNN
SORRY, GIRLS...
...BUT I DON'T HAVE TIME...
POIT
POIT
...TO CHAT RIGHT NOW.
TUMP
WE'LL CATCH UP LATER.

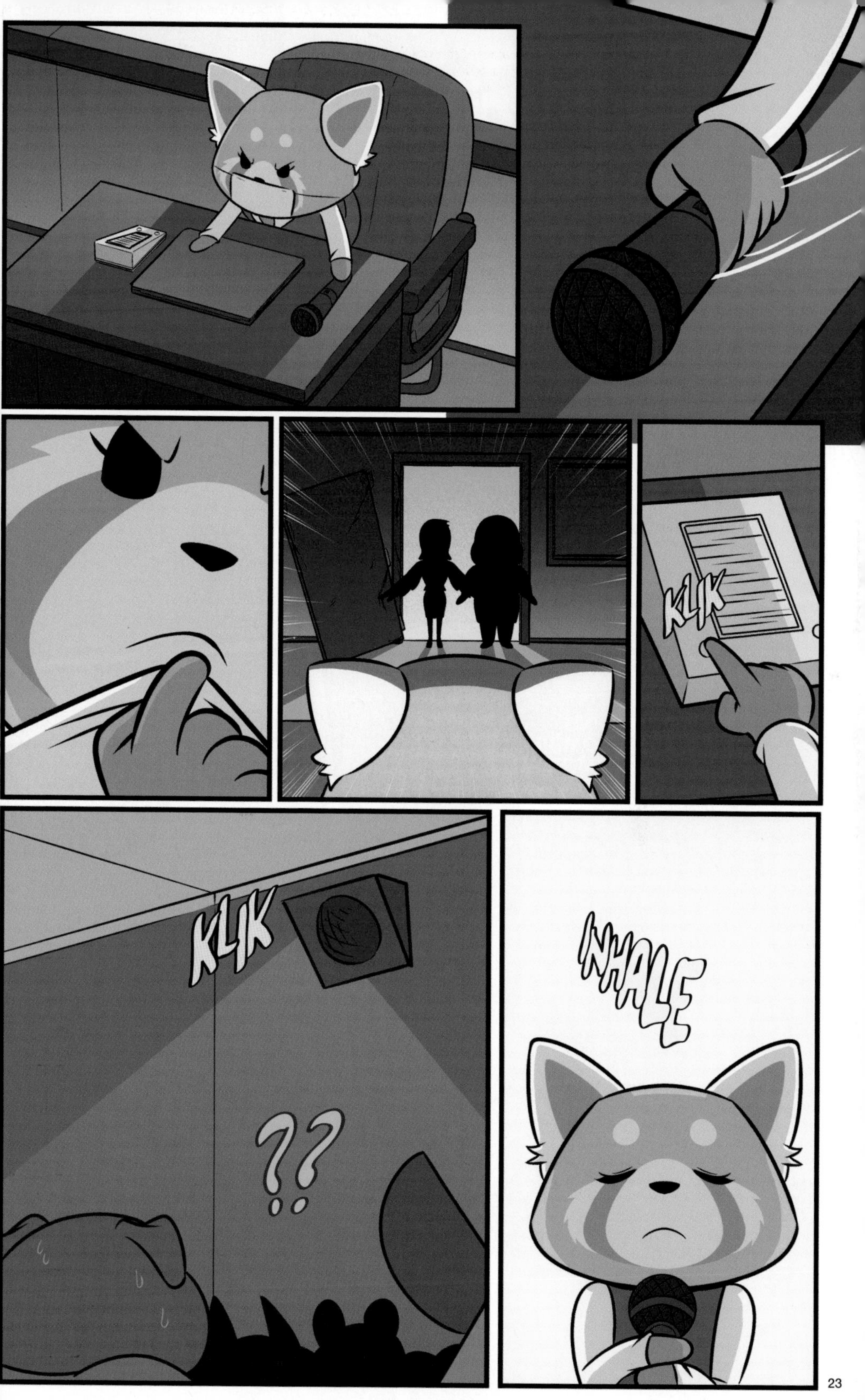
KLIK
KLIK
??
INHALE

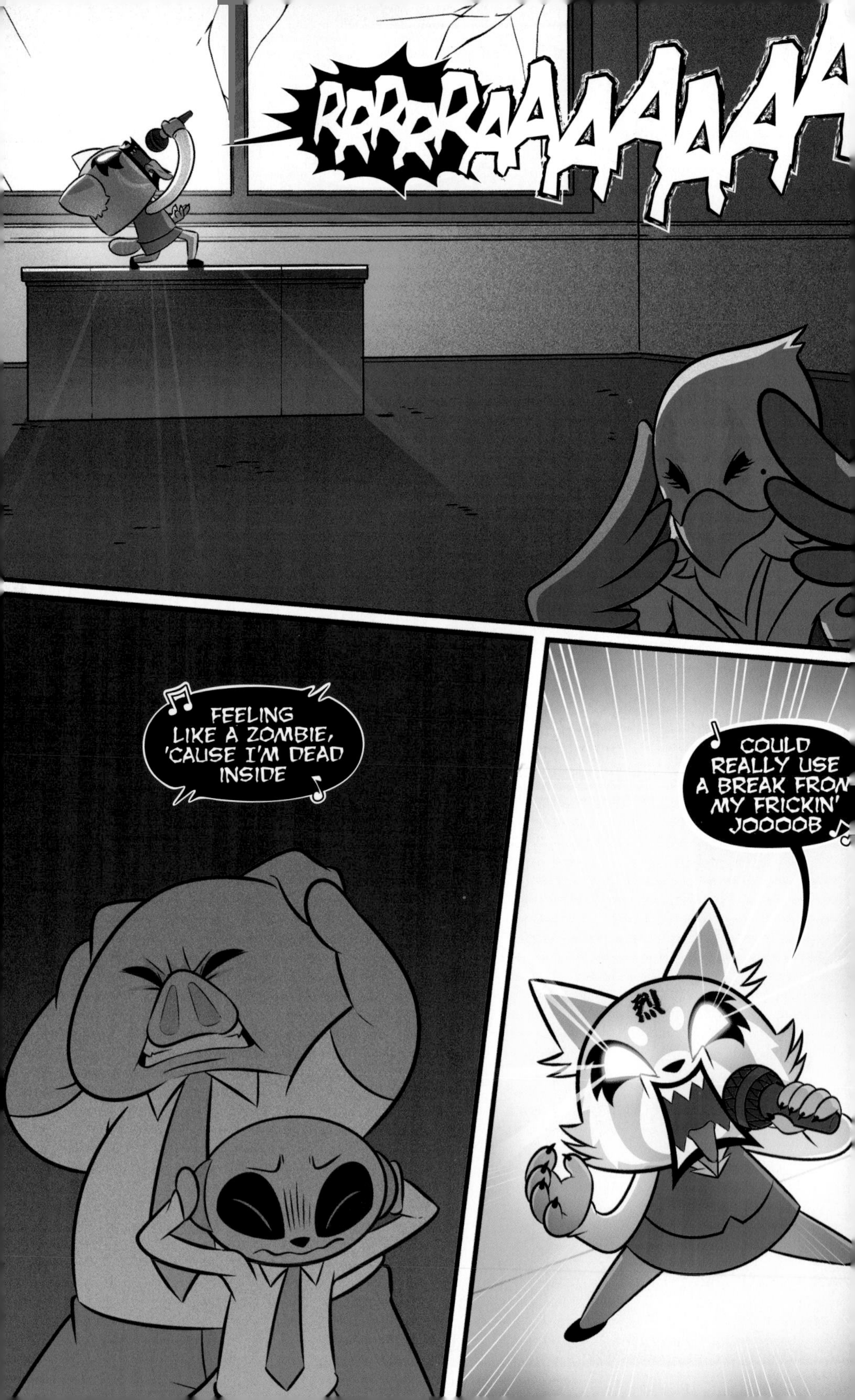
RRRRRAAAAAAA
FEELING LIKE A ZOMBIE, 'CAUSE I'M DEAD INSIDE
COULD REALLY USE A BREAK FROM MY FRICKIN' JOOOOB

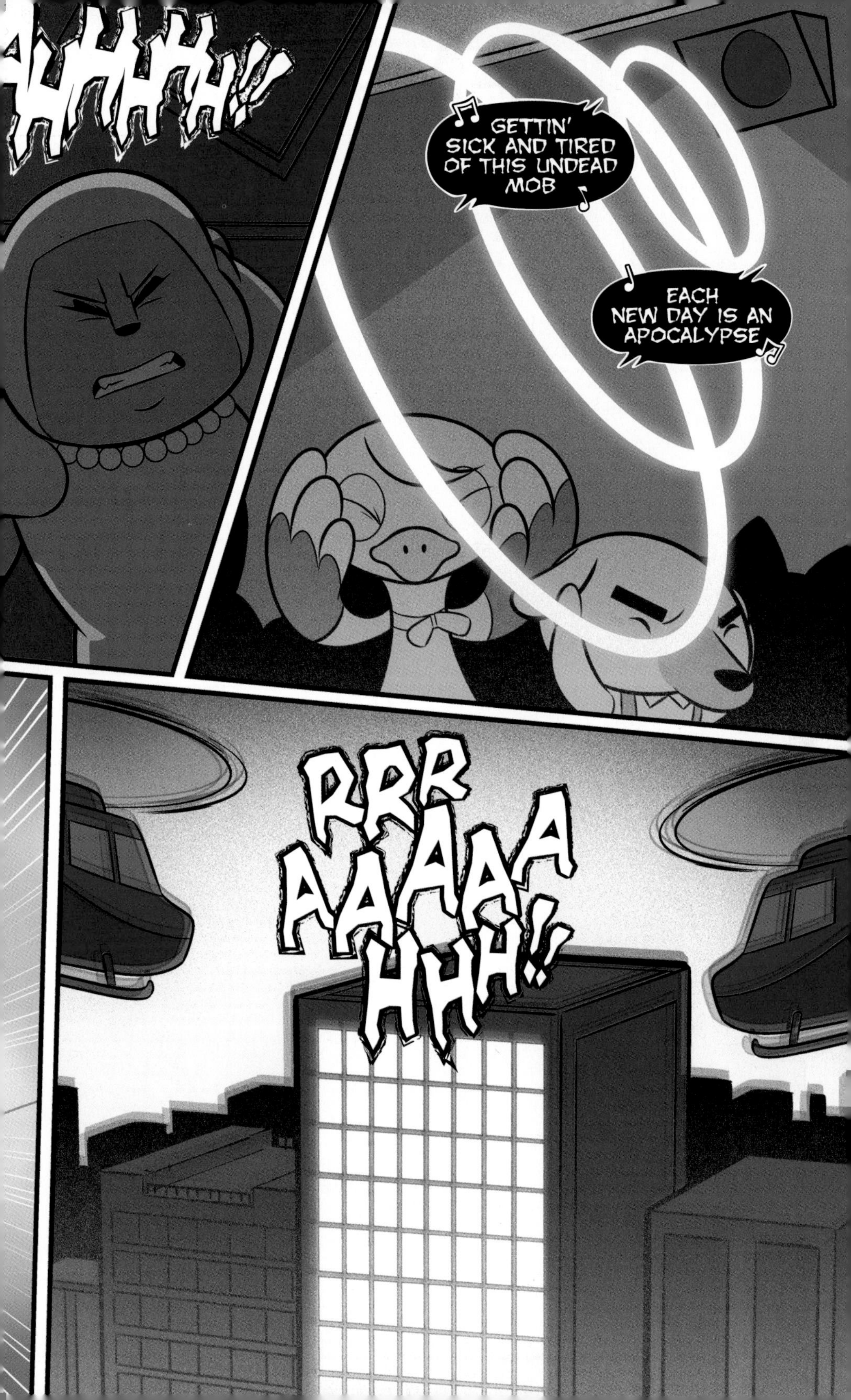
HHHHH!!
GETTIN' SICK AND TIRED OF THIS UNDEAD MOB
EACH NEW DAY IS AN APOCALYPSE
RRRAAAAAHHH!!

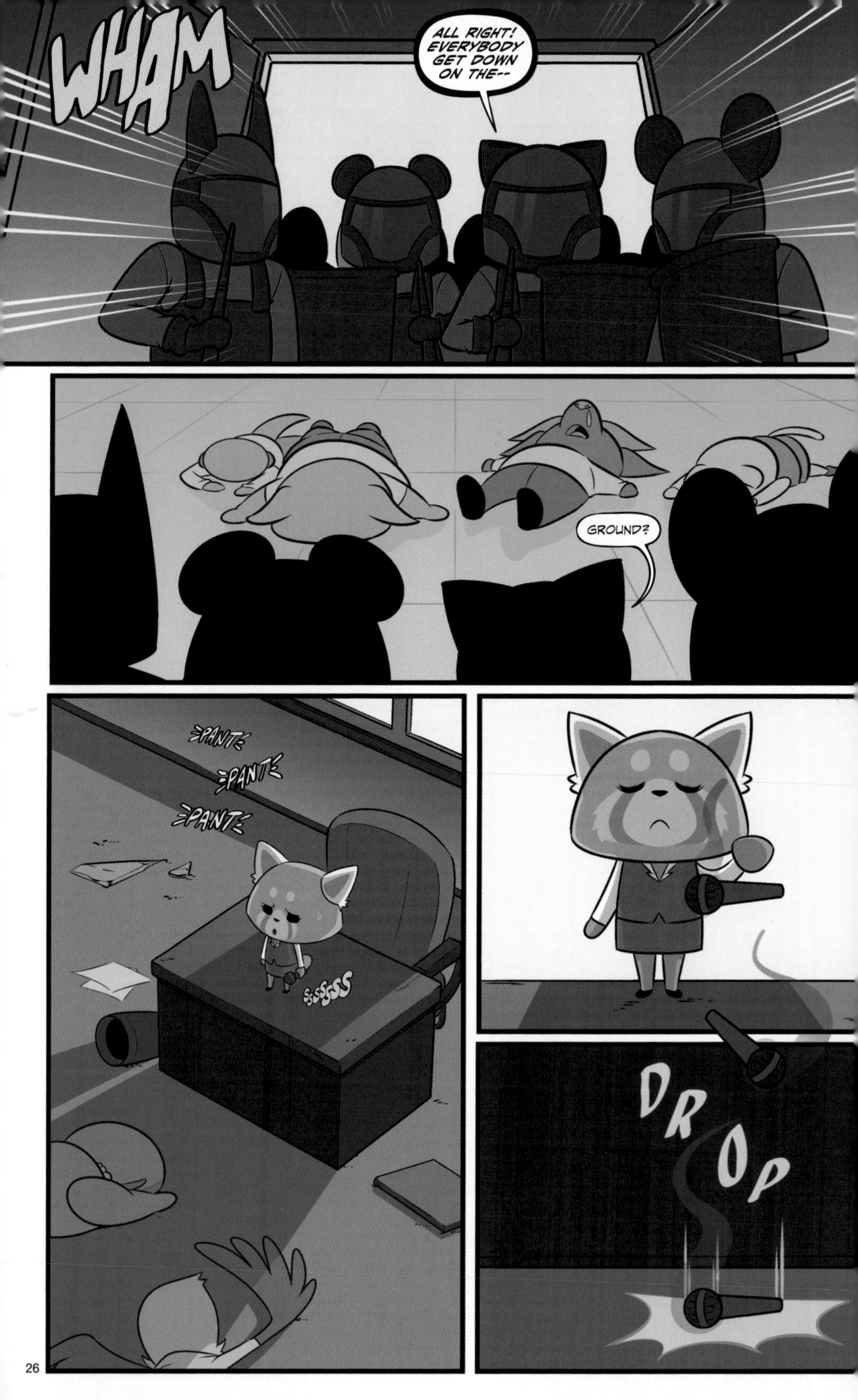
WHAM
ALL RIGHT! EVERYBODY GET DOWN ON THE--
GROUND?
PANT
PANT
PANT
SSSSSS
DROP

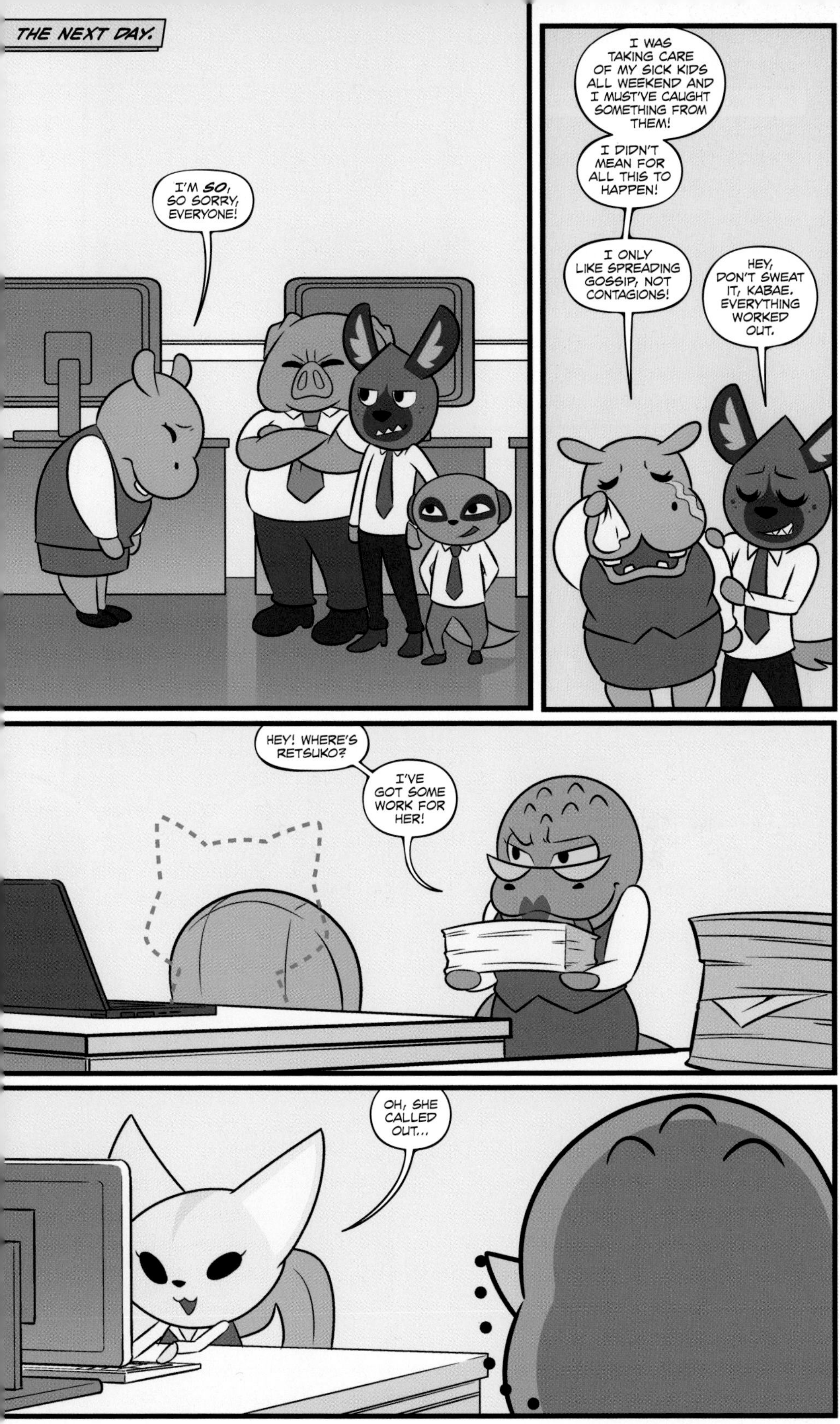
THE NEXT DAY.
I'M SO, SO SORRY, EVERYONE!
I WAS TAKING CARE OF MY SICK KIDS ALL WEEKEND AND I MUST'VE CAUGHT SOMETHING FROM THEM!
I DIDN'T MEAN FOR ALL THIS TO HAPPEN!
I ONLY LIKE SPREADING GOSSIP, NOT CONTAGIONS!
HEY, DON'T SWEAT IT, KABAE. EVERYTHING WORKED OUT.
HEY! WHERE'S RETSUKO?
I'VE GOT SOME WORK FOR HER!
OH, SHE CALLED OUT...

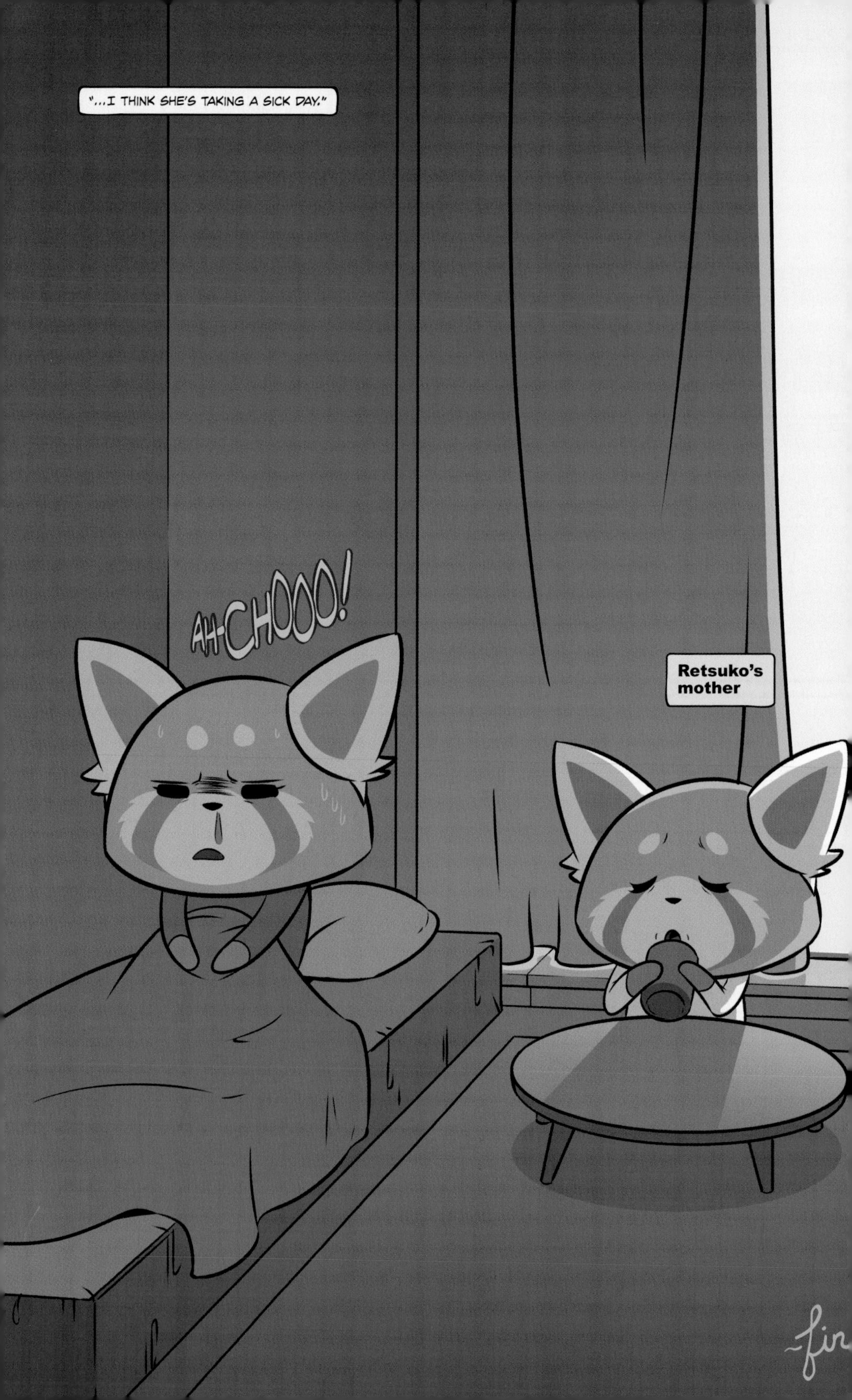
"...I THINK SHE'S TAKING A SICK DAY."
AH-CHOOO!
Retsuko's mother
-fin

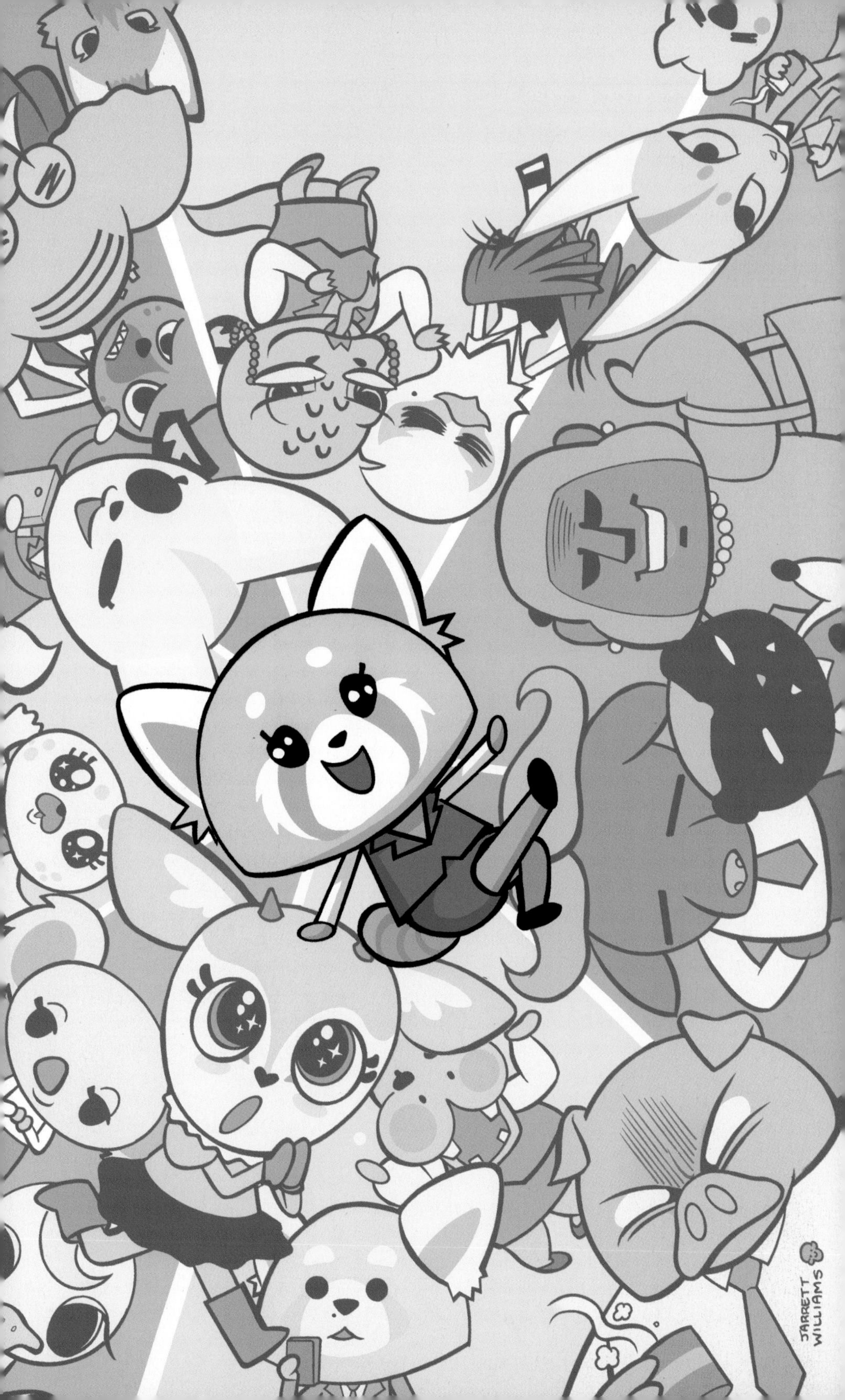
JARRETT WILLIAMS

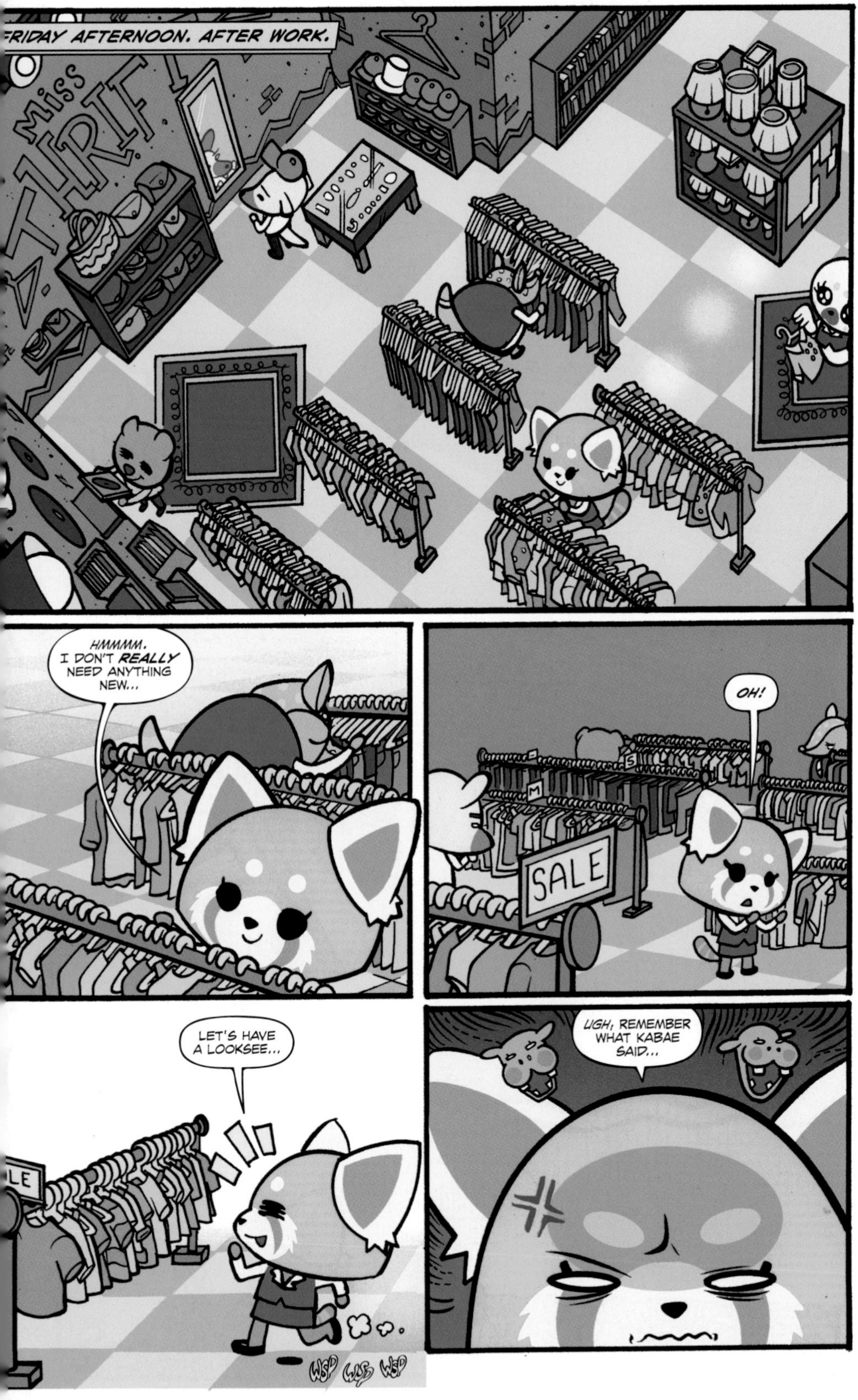
FRIDAY AFTERNOON. AFTER WORK.
HMMMM. I DON'T REALLY NEED ANYTHING NEW...
OH!
SALE
LET'S HAVE A LOOKSEE...
WSP WSP WSP
UGH, REMEMBER WHAT KABAE SAID...

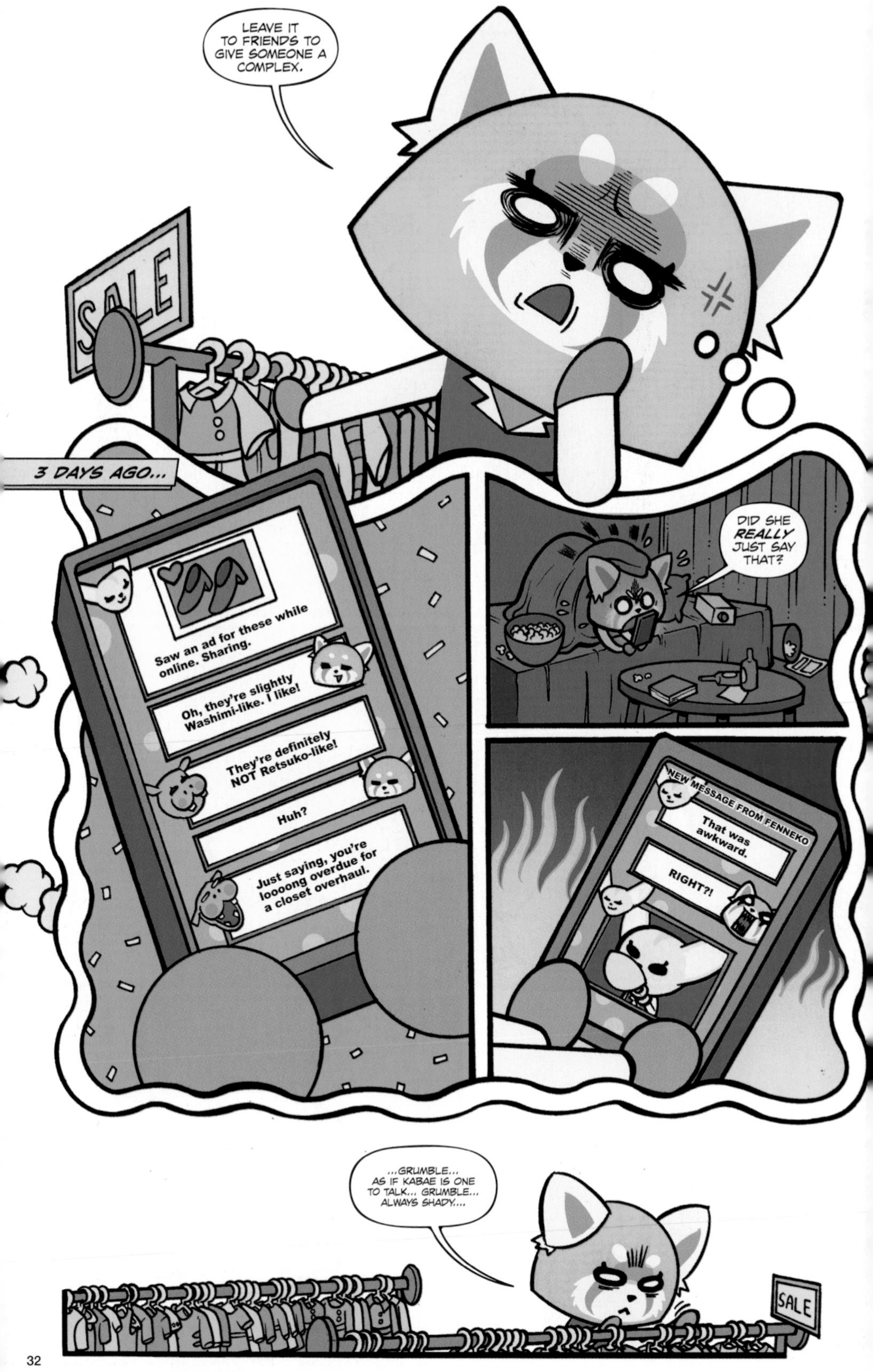
LEAVE IT TO FRIENDS TO GIVE SOMEONE A COMPLEX.
SALE
3 DAYS AGO...
Saw an ad for these while online. Sharing.
Oh, they're slightly Washimi-like. I like!
They're definitely NOT Retsuko-like!
Huh?
Just saying, you're loooong overdue for a closet overhaul.
DID SHE REALLY JUST SAY THAT?
NEW MESSAGE FROM FENNEKO
That was awkward.
RIGHT?!
...GRUMBLE... AS IF KABAE IS ONE TO TALK... GRUMBLE... ALWAYS SHADY....
SALE

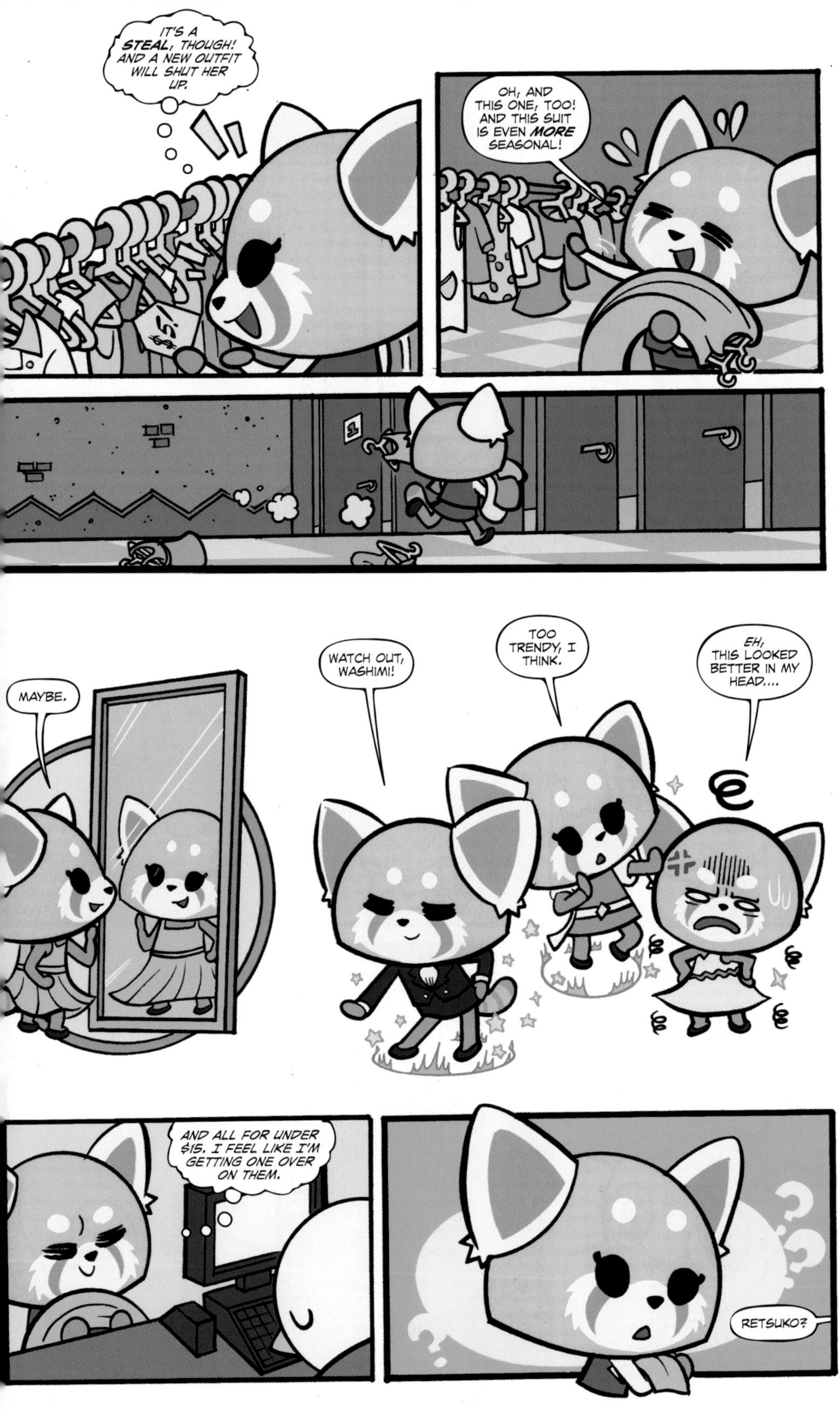

IT'S A STEAL, THOUGH! AND A NEW OUTFIT WILL SHUT HER UP.
$15!
OH, AND THIS ONE, TOO! AND THIS SUIT IS EVEN MORE SEASONAL!
MAYBE.
WATCH OUT, WASHIMI!
TOO TRENDY, I THINK.
EH, THIS LOOKED BETTER IN MY HEAD....
AND ALL FOR UNDER $15. I FEEL LIKE I'M GETTING ONE OVER ON THEM.
RETSUKO?

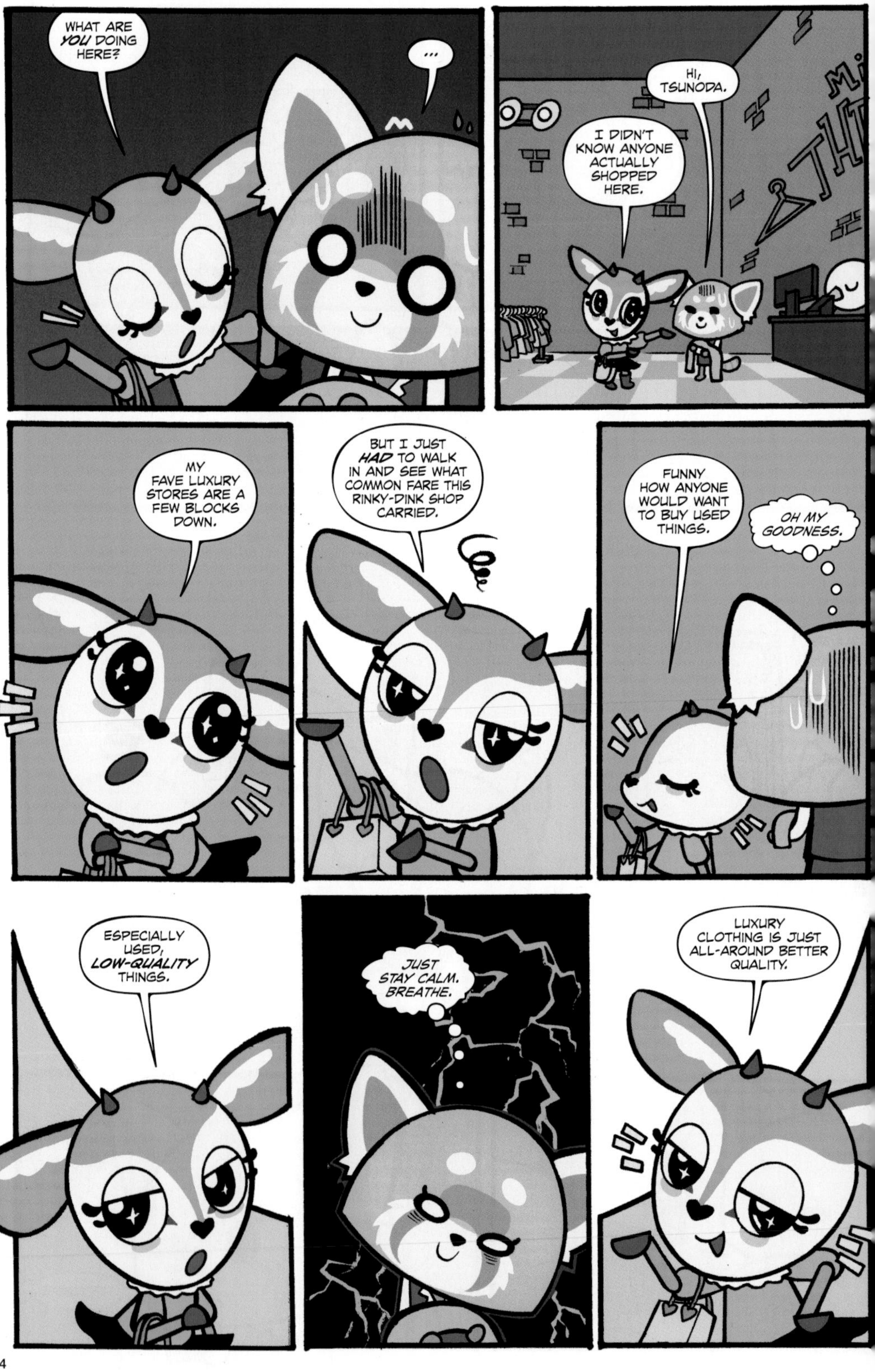
WHAT ARE *YOU* DOING HERE?
...
HI, TSUNODA.
I DIDN'T KNOW ANYONE ACTUALLY SHOPPED HERE.
MY FAVE LUXURY STORES ARE A FEW BLOCKS DOWN.
BUT I JUST ***HAD*** TO WALK IN AND SEE WHAT COMMON FARE THIS RINKY-DINK SHOP CARRIED.
FUNNY HOW ANYONE WOULD WANT TO BUY USED THINGS.
OH MY GOODNESS.
ESPECIALLY USED, ***LOW-QUALITY*** THINGS.
JUST STAY CALM. BREATHE.
LUXURY CLOTHING IS JUST ALL-AROUND BETTER QUALITY.

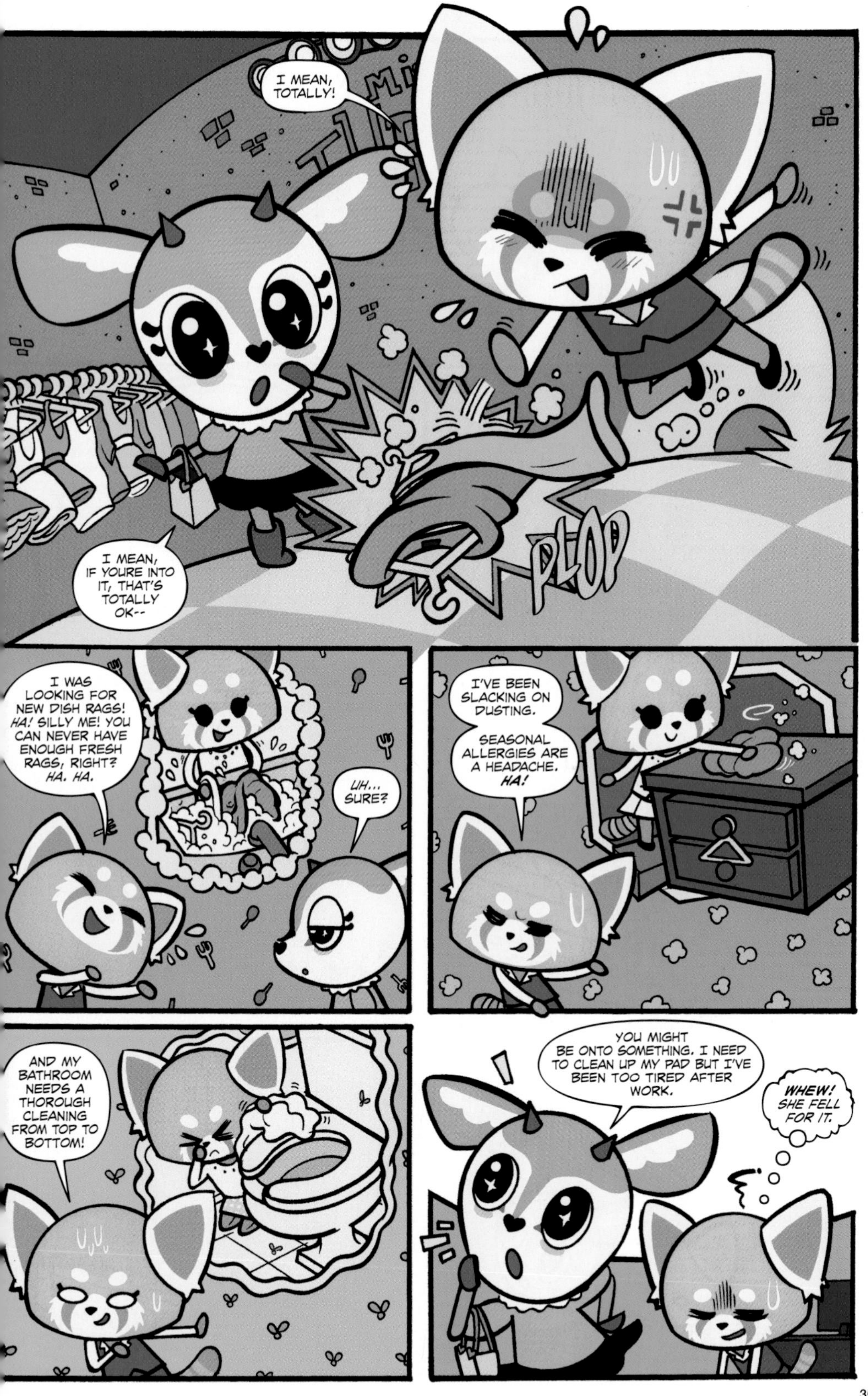
I MEAN, TOTALLY!
I MEAN, IF YOURE INTO IT, THAT'S TOTALLY OK--
PLOP
I WAS LOOKING FOR NEW DISH RAGS! HA! SILLY ME! YOU CAN NEVER HAVE ENOUGH FRESH RAGS, RIGHT? HA. HA.
UH... SURE?
I'VE BEEN SLACKING ON DUSTING.
SEASONAL ALLERGIES ARE A HEADACHE. HA!
AND MY BATHROOM NEEDS A THOROUGH CLEANING FROM TOP TO BOTTOM!
YOU MIGHT BE ONTO SOMETHING. I NEED TO CLEAN UP MY PAD BUT I'VE BEEN TOO TIRED AFTER WORK.
WHEW! SHE FELL FOR IT.

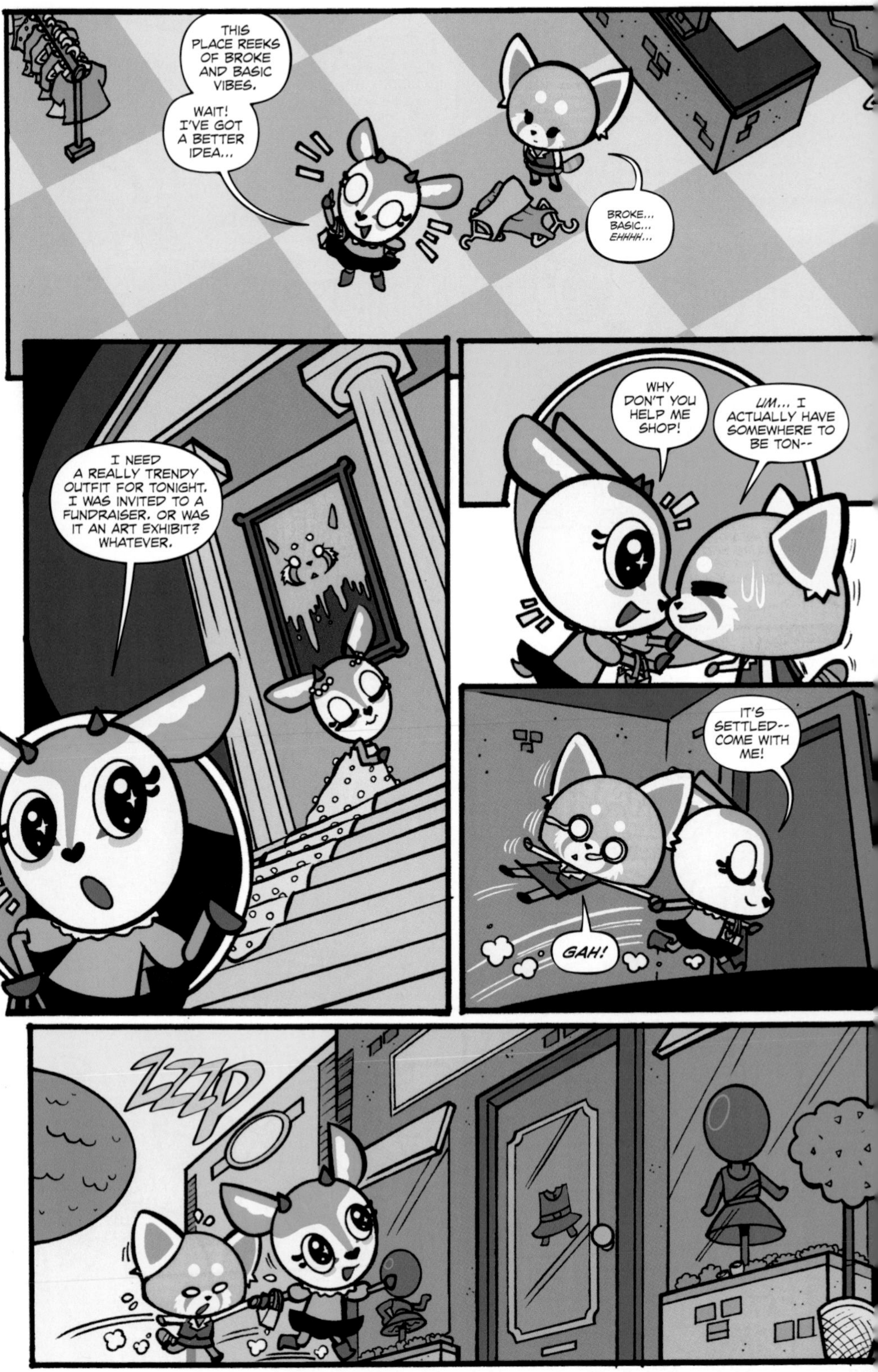
THIS PLACE REEKS OF BROKE AND BASIC VIBES.
WAIT! I'VE GOT A BETTER IDEA...
BROKE... BASIC... *EHHHH*...
I NEED A REALLY TRENDY OUTFIT FOR TONIGHT. I WAS INVITED TO A FUNDRAISER. OR WAS IT AN ART EXHIBIT? WHATEVER.
WHY DON'T YOU HELP ME SHOP!
UM... I ACTUALLY HAVE SOMEWHERE TO BE TON--
IT'S SETTLED-- COME WITH ME!
GAH!
ZZZD

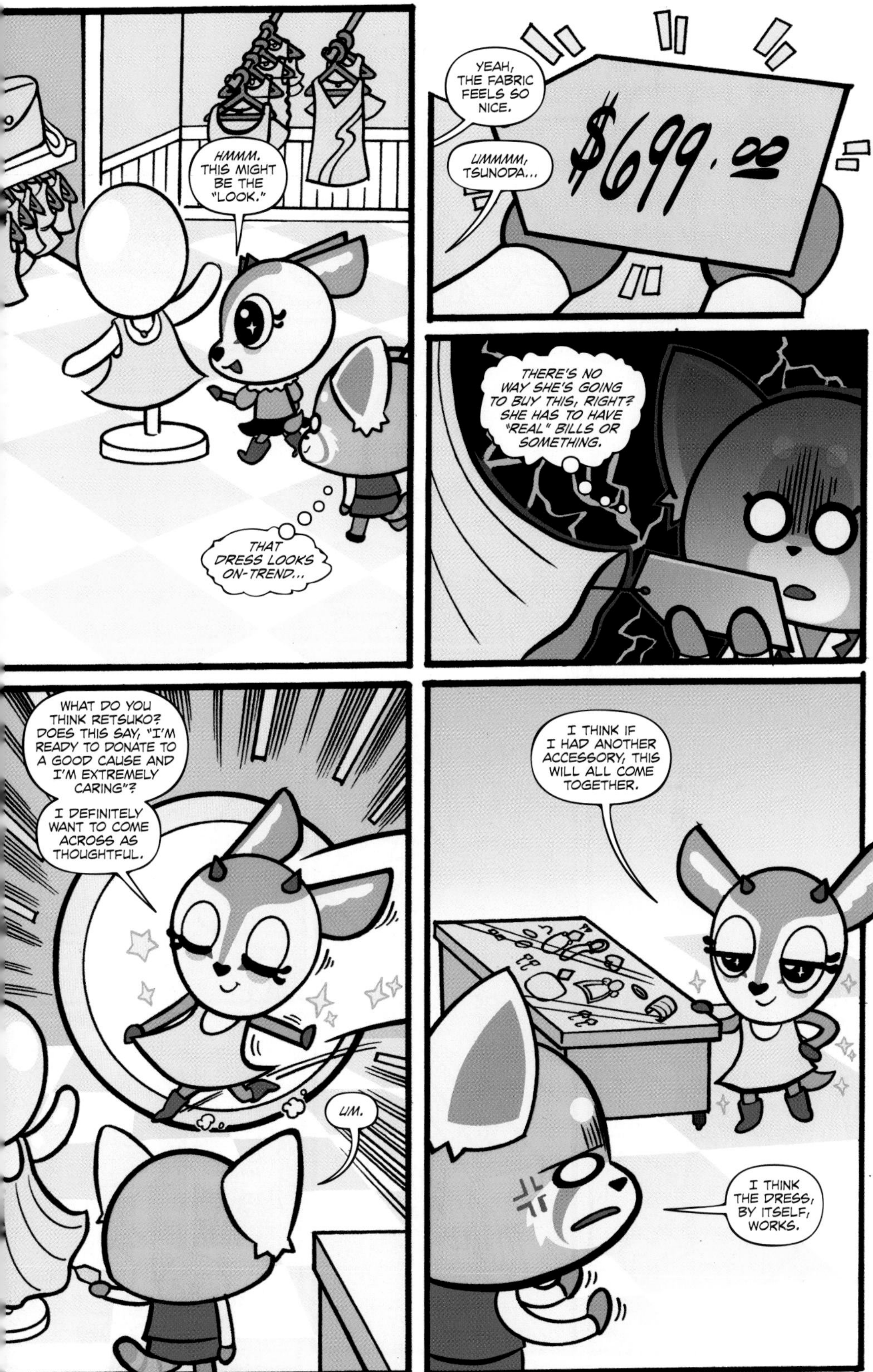
HMMM. THIS MIGHT BE THE "LOOK."
THAT DRESS LOOKS ON-TREND...
YEAH, THE FABRIC FEELS SO NICE.
UMMMM, TSUNODA...
$699.00
THERE'S NO WAY SHE'S GOING TO BUY THIS, RIGHT? SHE HAS TO HAVE "REAL" BILLS OR SOMETHING.
WHAT DO YOU THINK RETSUKO? DOES THIS SAY, "I'M READY TO DONATE TO A GOOD CAUSE AND I'M EXTREMELY CARING"?
I DEFINITELY WANT TO COME ACROSS AS THOUGHTFUL.
UM.
I THINK IF I HAD ANOTHER ACCESSORY, THIS WILL ALL COME TOGETHER.
I THINK THE DRESS, BY ITSELF, WORKS.

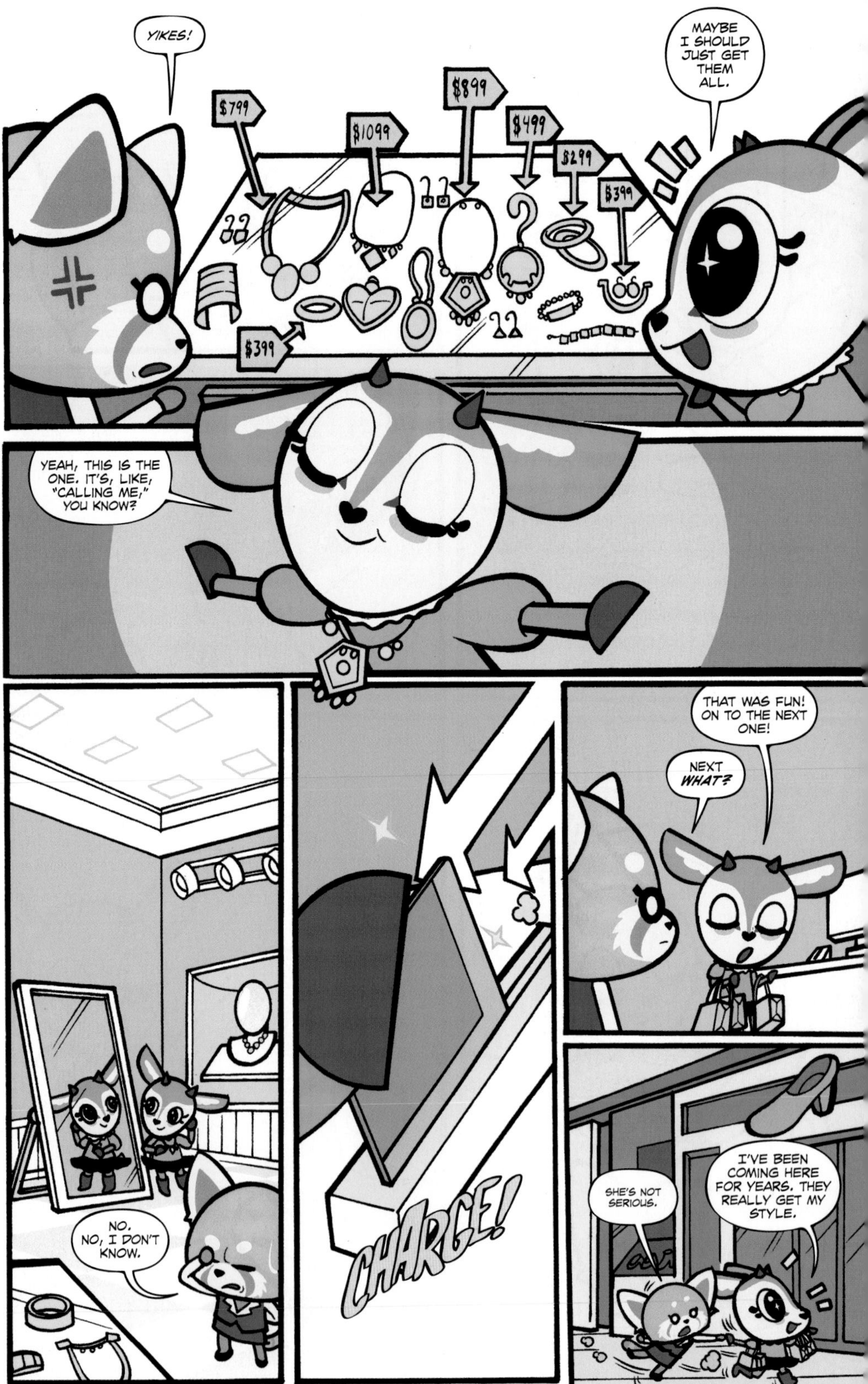
YIKES!
MAYBE I SHOULD JUST GET THEM ALL.
$799
$1099
$899
$499
$299
$399
$399
YEAH, THIS IS THE ONE. IT'S, LIKE, "CALLING ME," YOU KNOW?
NO. NO, I DON'T KNOW.
CHARGE!
THAT WAS FUN! ON TO THE NEXT ONE!
NEXT WHAT?
I'VE BEEN COMING HERE FOR YEARS. THEY REALLY GET MY STYLE.
SHE'S NOT SERIOUS.

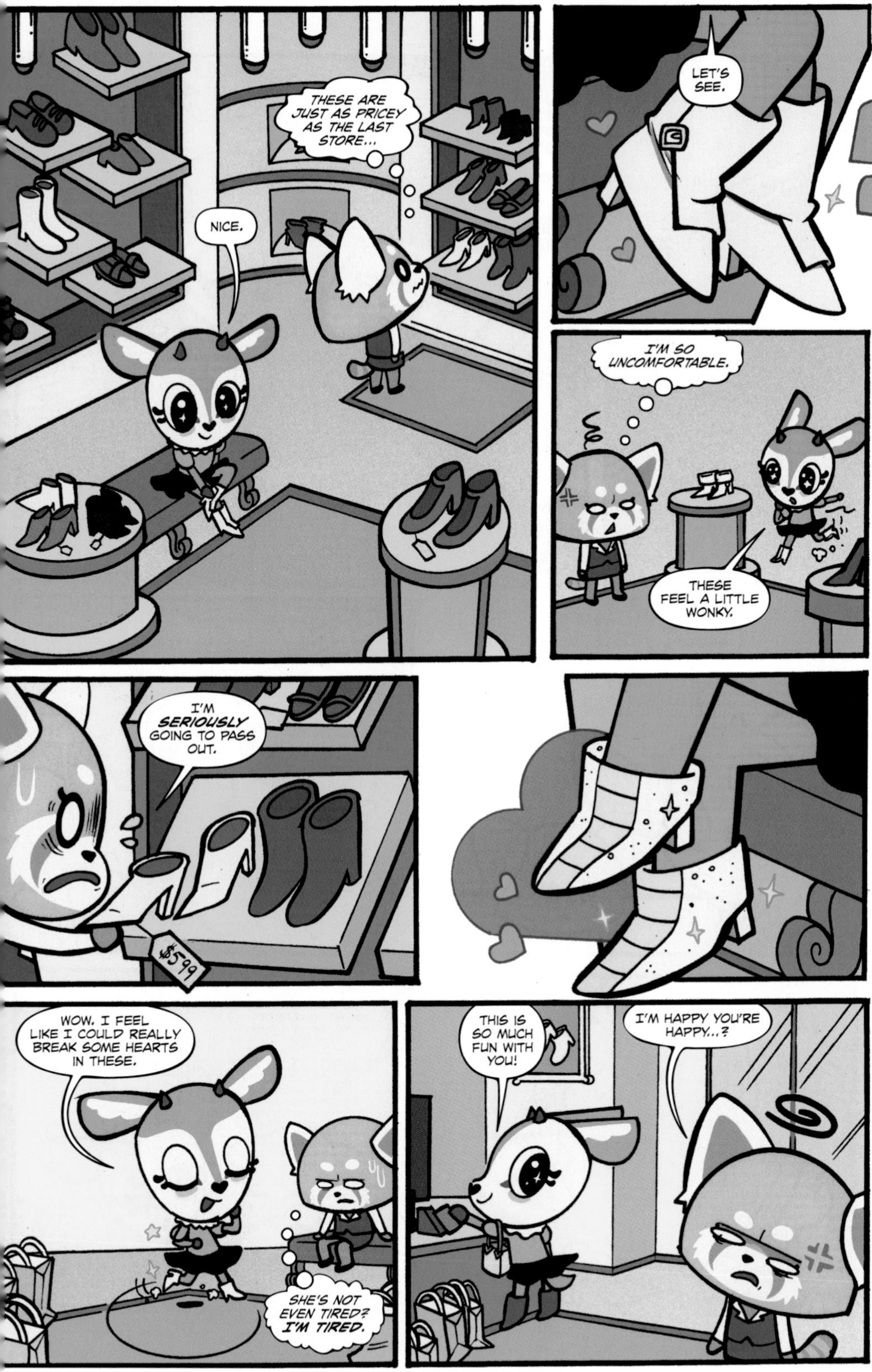
THESE ARE JUST AS PRICEY AS THE LAST STORE...
NICE.
LET'S SEE.
I'M SO UNCOMFORTABLE.
THESE FEEL A LITTLE WONKY.
I'M SERIOUSLY GOING TO PASS OUT.
$599
WOW. I FEEL LIKE I COULD REALLY BREAK SOME HEARTS IN THESE.
SHE'S NOT EVEN TIRED? I'M TIRED.
THIS IS SO MUCH FUN WITH YOU!
I'M HAPPY YOU'RE HAPPY...?

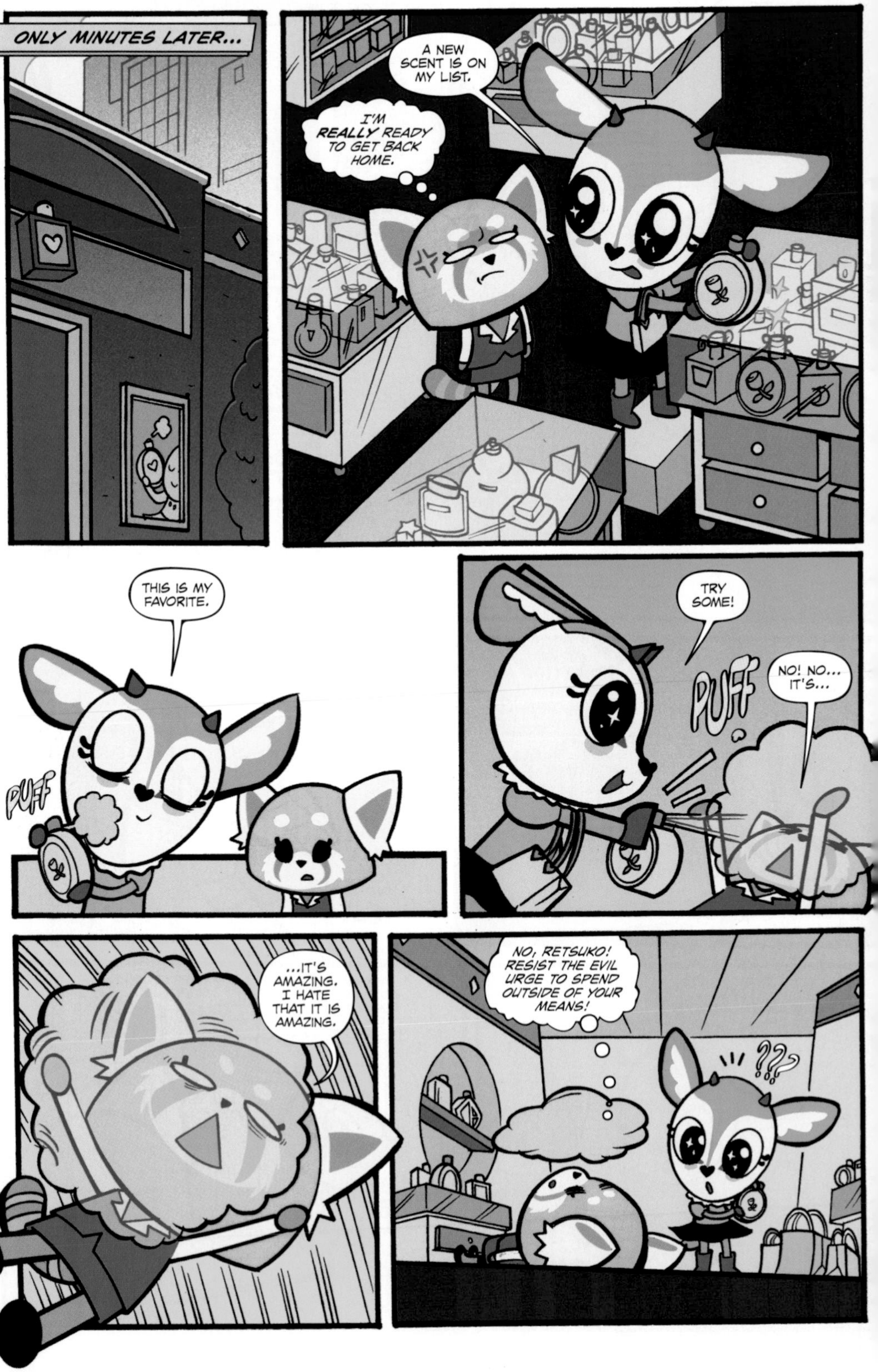
ONLY MINUTES LATER...
A NEW SCENT IS ON MY LIST.
I'M REALLY READY TO GET BACK HOME.
THIS IS MY FAVORITE.
PUFF
TRY SOME!
PUFF
NO! NO... IT'S...
...IT'S AMAZING. I HATE THAT IT IS AMAZING.
NO, RETSUKO! RESIST THE EVIL URGE TO SPEND OUTSIDE OF YOUR MEANS!
???

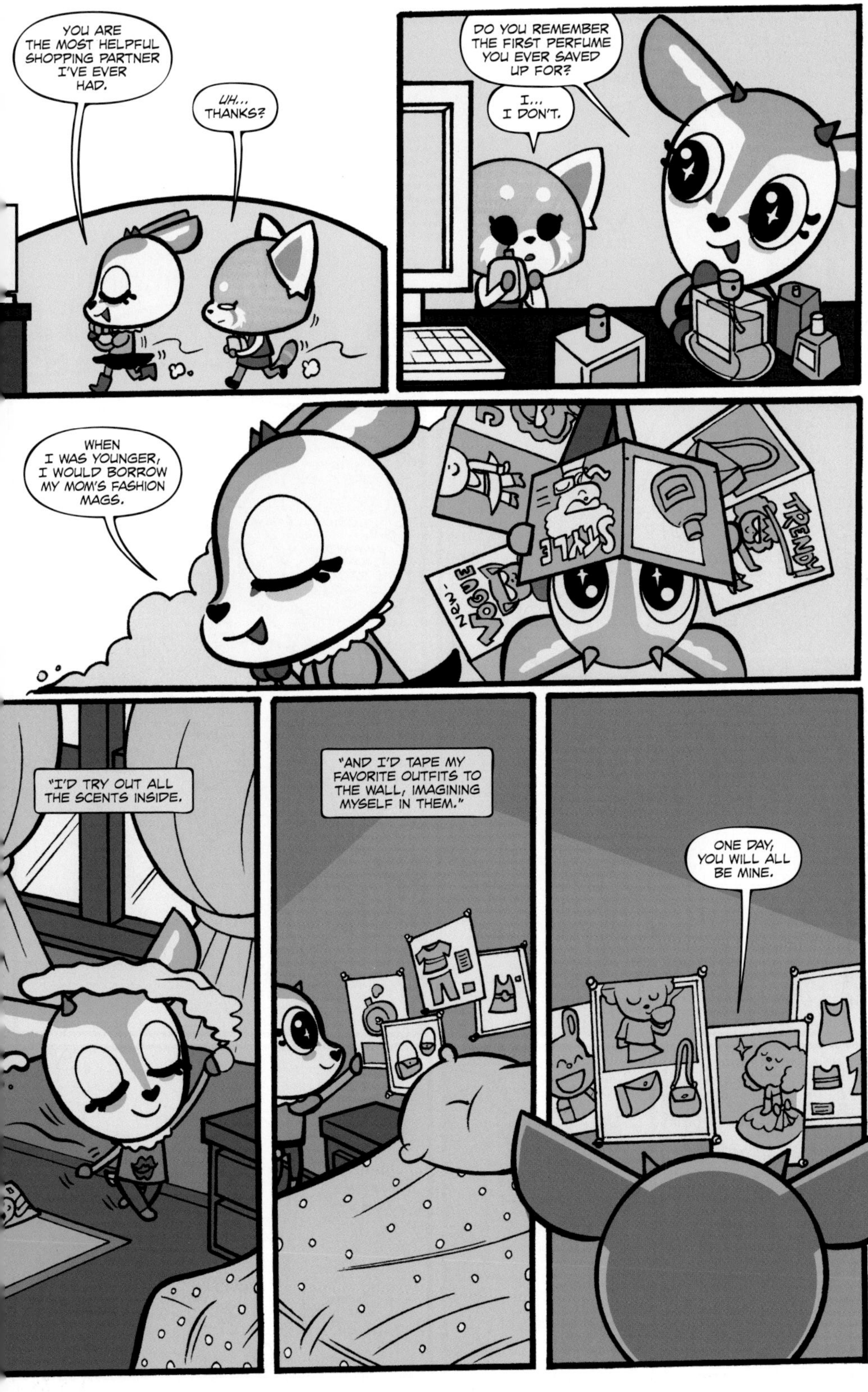
YOU ARE THE MOST HELPFUL SHOPPING PARTNER I'VE EVER HAD.
UH... THANKS?
DO YOU REMEMBER THE FIRST PERFUME YOU EVER SAVED UP FOR?
I... I DON'T.
WHEN I WAS YOUNGER, I WOULD BORROW MY MOM'S FASHION MAGS.
STYLE
TRENDY
NEW
VOGUE
"I'D TRY OUT ALL THE SCENTS INSIDE.
"AND I'D TAPE MY FAVORITE OUTFITS TO THE WALL, IMAGINING MYSELF IN THEM."
ONE DAY, YOU WILL ALL BE MINE.

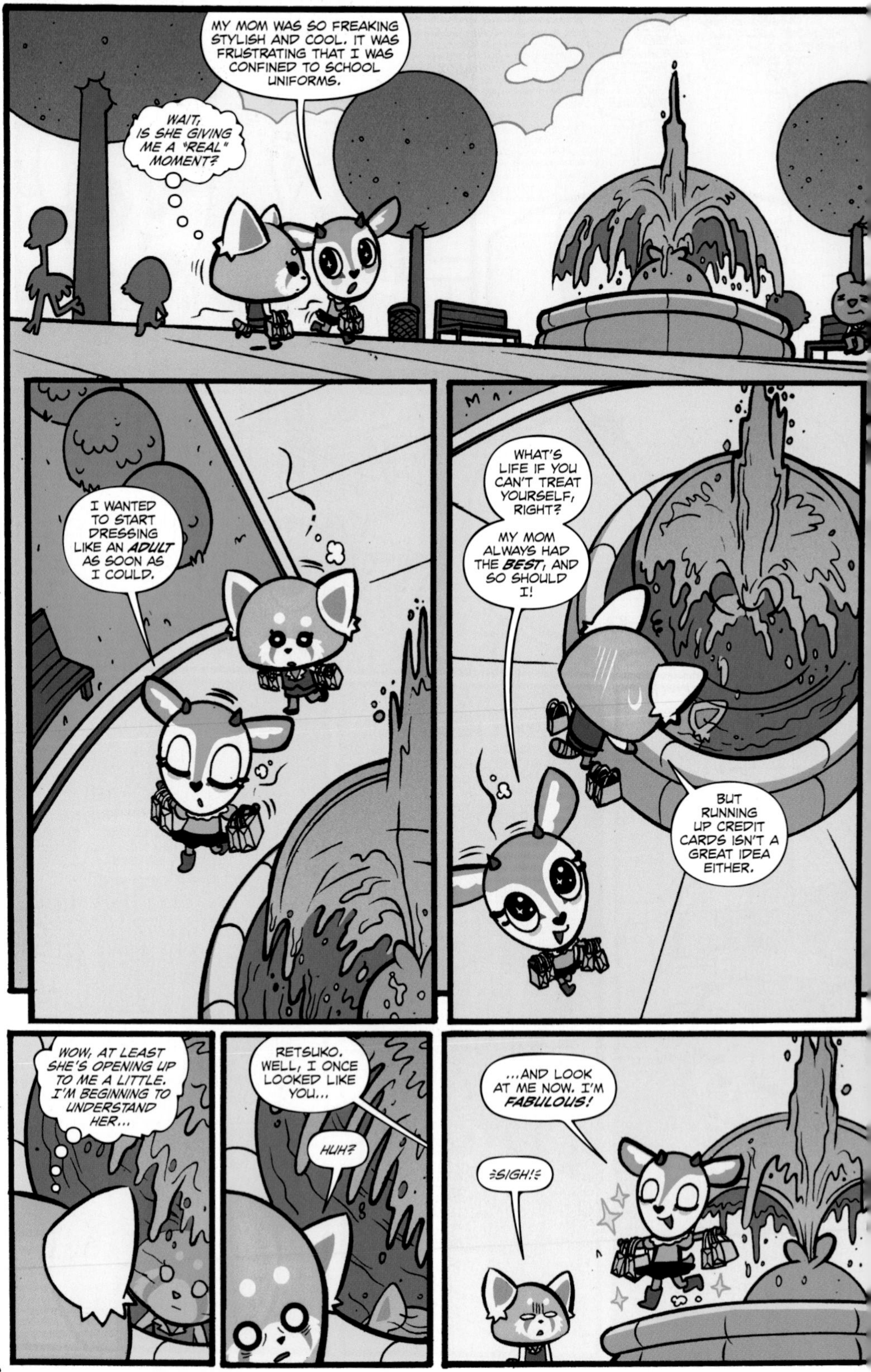
MY MOM WAS SO FREAKING STYLISH AND COOL. IT WAS FRUSTRATING THAT I WAS CONFINED TO SCHOOL UNIFORMS.
WAIT, IS SHE GIVING ME A "REAL" MOMENT?
I WANTED TO START DRESSING LIKE AN ADULT AS SOON AS I COULD.
WHAT'S LIFE IF YOU CAN'T TREAT YOURSELF, RIGHT?
MY MOM ALWAYS HAD THE BEST, AND SO SHOULD I!
BUT RUNNING UP CREDIT CARDS ISN'T A GREAT IDEA EITHER.
WOW, AT LEAST SHE'S OPENING UP TO ME A LITTLE. I'M BEGINNING TO UNDERSTAND HER...
RETSUKO. WELL, I ONCE LOOKED LIKE YOU...
HUH?
...AND LOOK AT ME NOW. I'M FABULOUS!
SIGH!

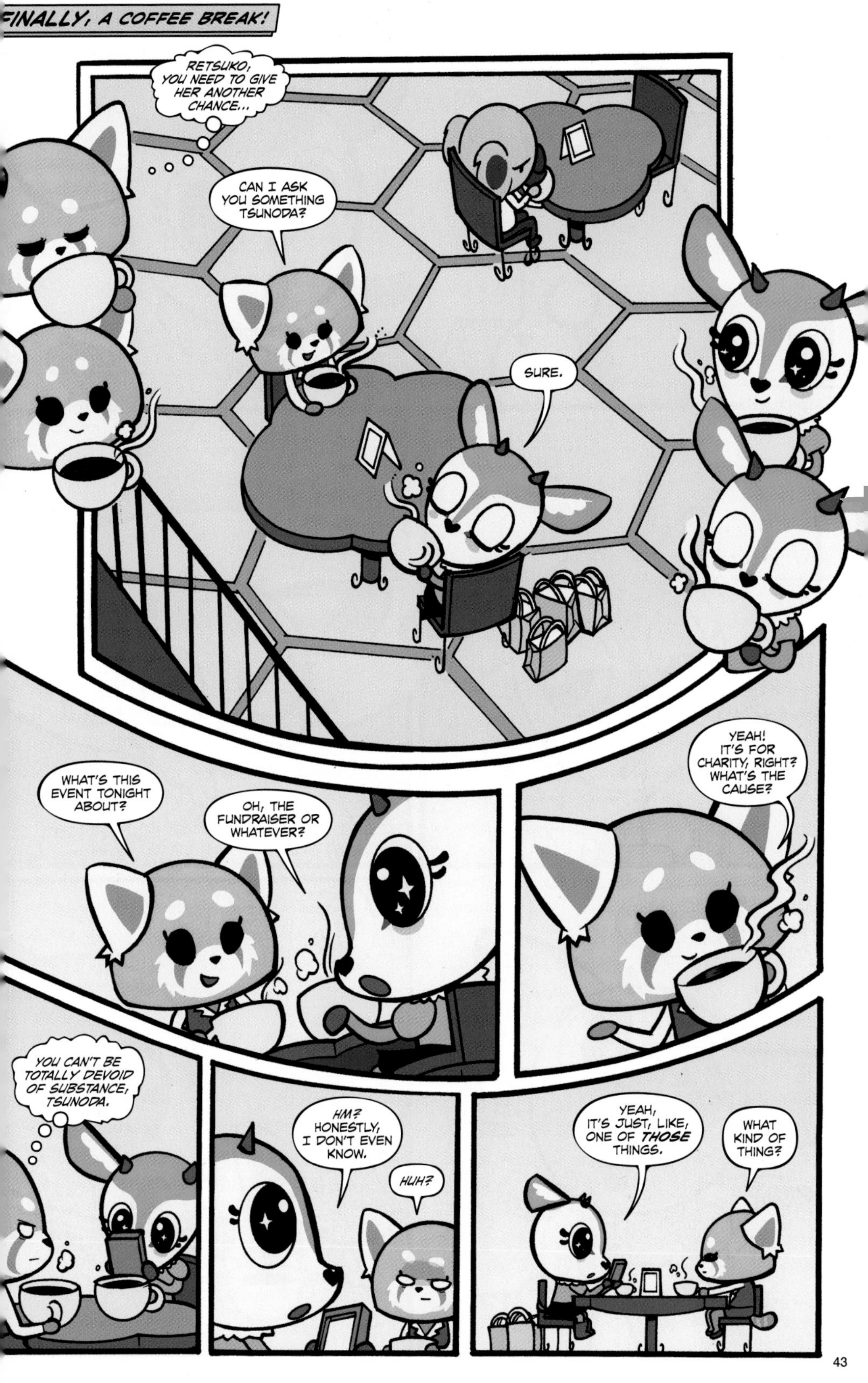
FINALLY, A COFFEE BREAK!
RETSUKO, YOU NEED TO GIVE HER ANOTHER CHANCE...
CAN I ASK YOU SOMETHING TSUNODA?
SURE.
WHAT'S THIS EVENT TONIGHT ABOUT?
OH, THE FUNDRAISER OR WHATEVER?
YEAH! IT'S FOR CHARITY, RIGHT? WHAT'S THE CAUSE?
YOU CAN'T BE TOTALLY DEVOID OF SUBSTANCE, TSUNODA.
HM? HONESTLY, I DON'T EVEN KNOW.
HUH?
YEAH, IT'S JUST, LIKE, ONE OF *THOSE* THINGS.
WHAT KIND OF THING?

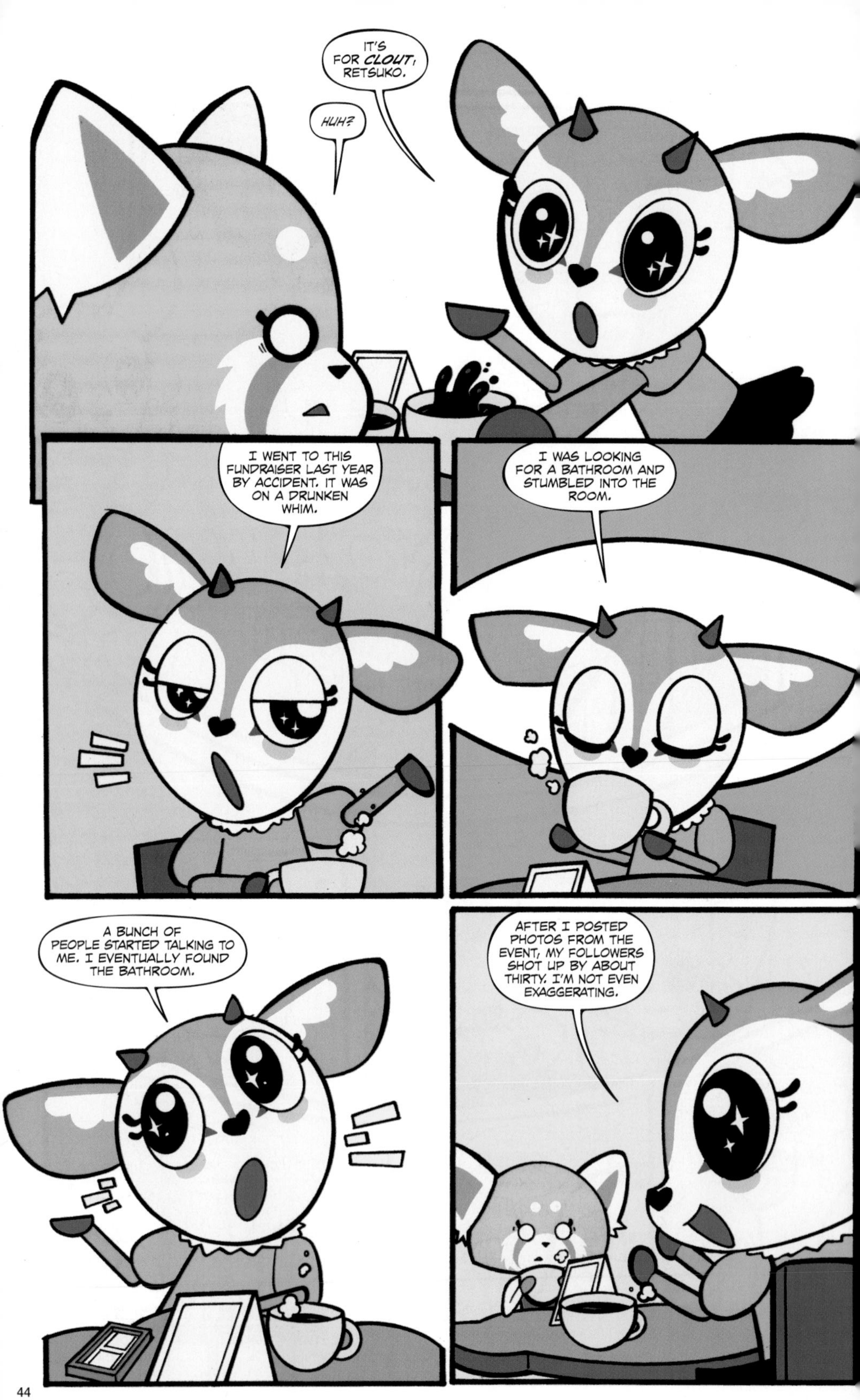
HUH?
IT'S FOR *CLOUT*, RETSUKO.
I WENT TO THIS FUNDRAISER LAST YEAR BY ACCIDENT. IT WAS ON A DRUNKEN WHIM.
I WAS LOOKING FOR A BATHROOM AND STUMBLED INTO THE ROOM.
A BUNCH OF PEOPLE STARTED TALKING TO ME. I EVENTUALLY FOUND THE BATHROOM.
AFTER I POSTED PHOTOS FROM THE EVENT, MY FOLLOWERS SHOT UP BY ABOUT THIRTY. I'M NOT EVEN EXAGGERATING.

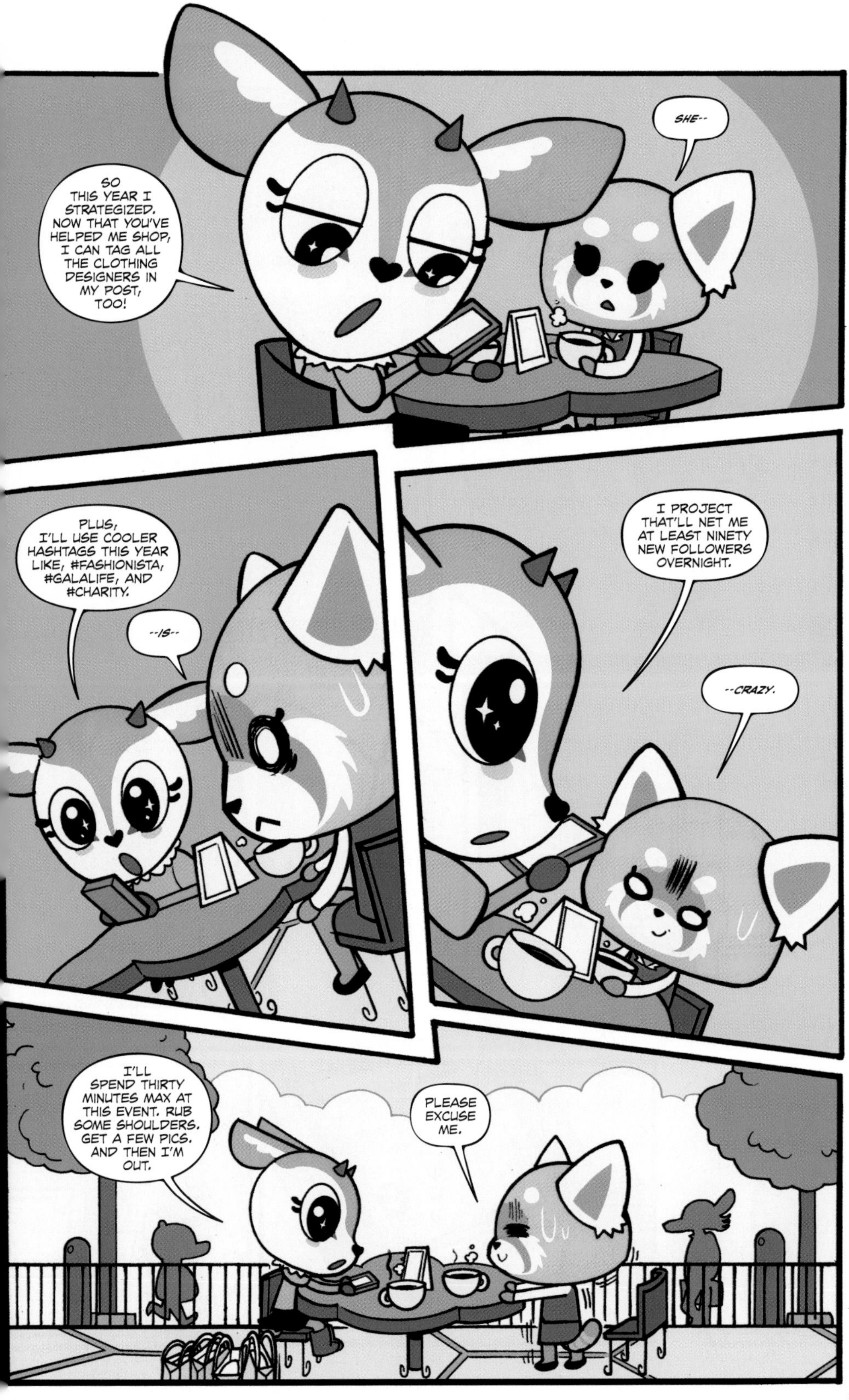
SO THIS YEAR I STRATEGIZED. NOW THAT YOU'VE HELPED ME SHOP, I CAN TAG ALL THE CLOTHING DESIGNERS IN MY POST, TOO!
SHE--
PLUS, I'LL USE COOLER HASHTAGS THIS YEAR LIKE, #FASHIONISTA, #GALALIFE, AND #CHARITY.
--IS--
I PROJECT THAT'LL NET ME AT LEAST NINETY NEW FOLLOWERS OVERNIGHT.
--CRAZY.
I'LL SPEND THIRTY MINUTES MAX AT THIS EVENT. RUB SOME SHOULDERS. GET A FEW PICS. AND THEN I'M OUT.
PLEASE EXCUSE ME.

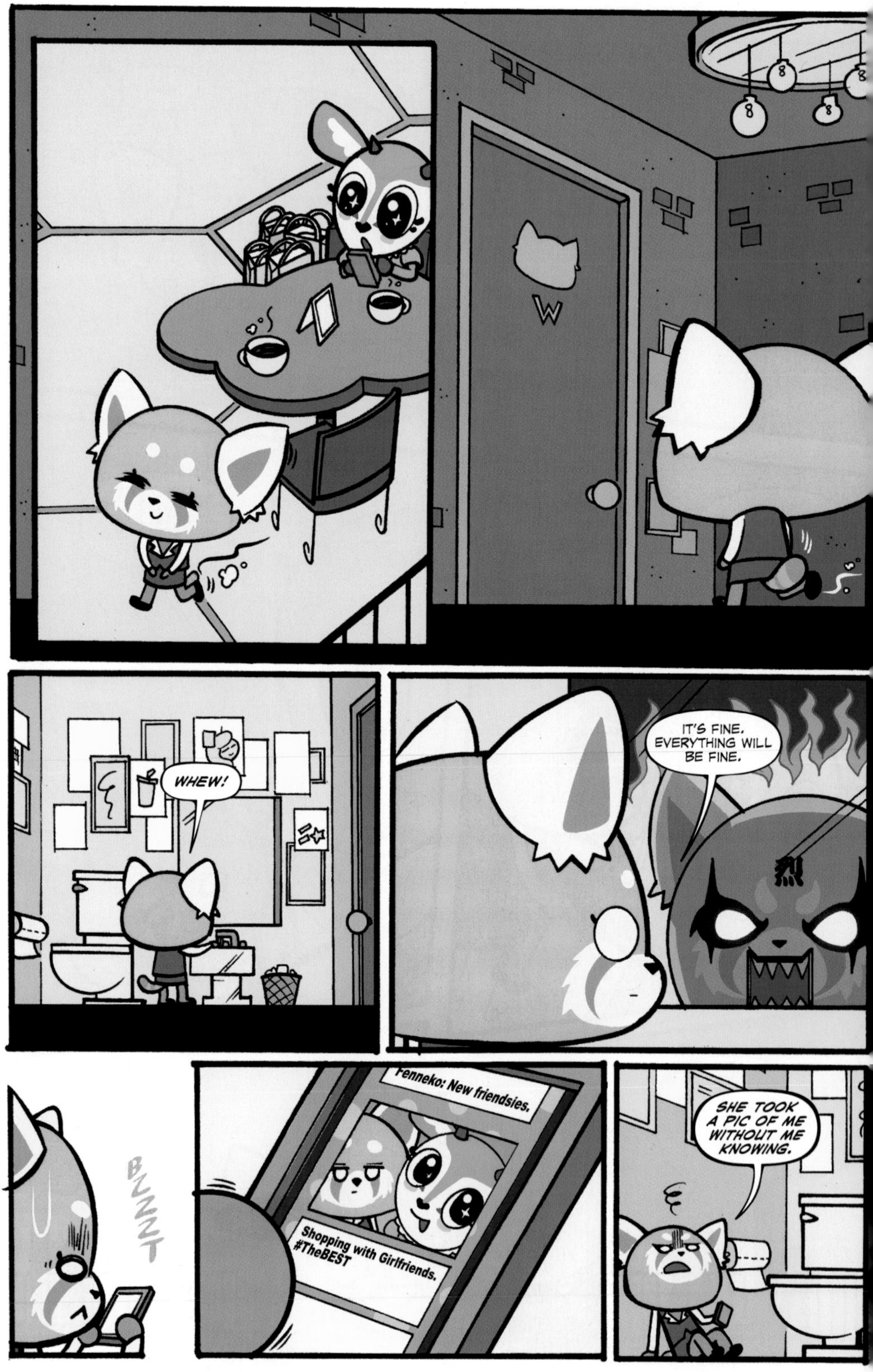
W
WHEW!
IT'S FINE. EVERYTHING WILL BE FINE.
BZZZT
Fenneko: New friendsies.
Shopping with Girlfriends. #TheBEST
SHE TOOK A PIC OF ME WITHOUT ME KNOWING.

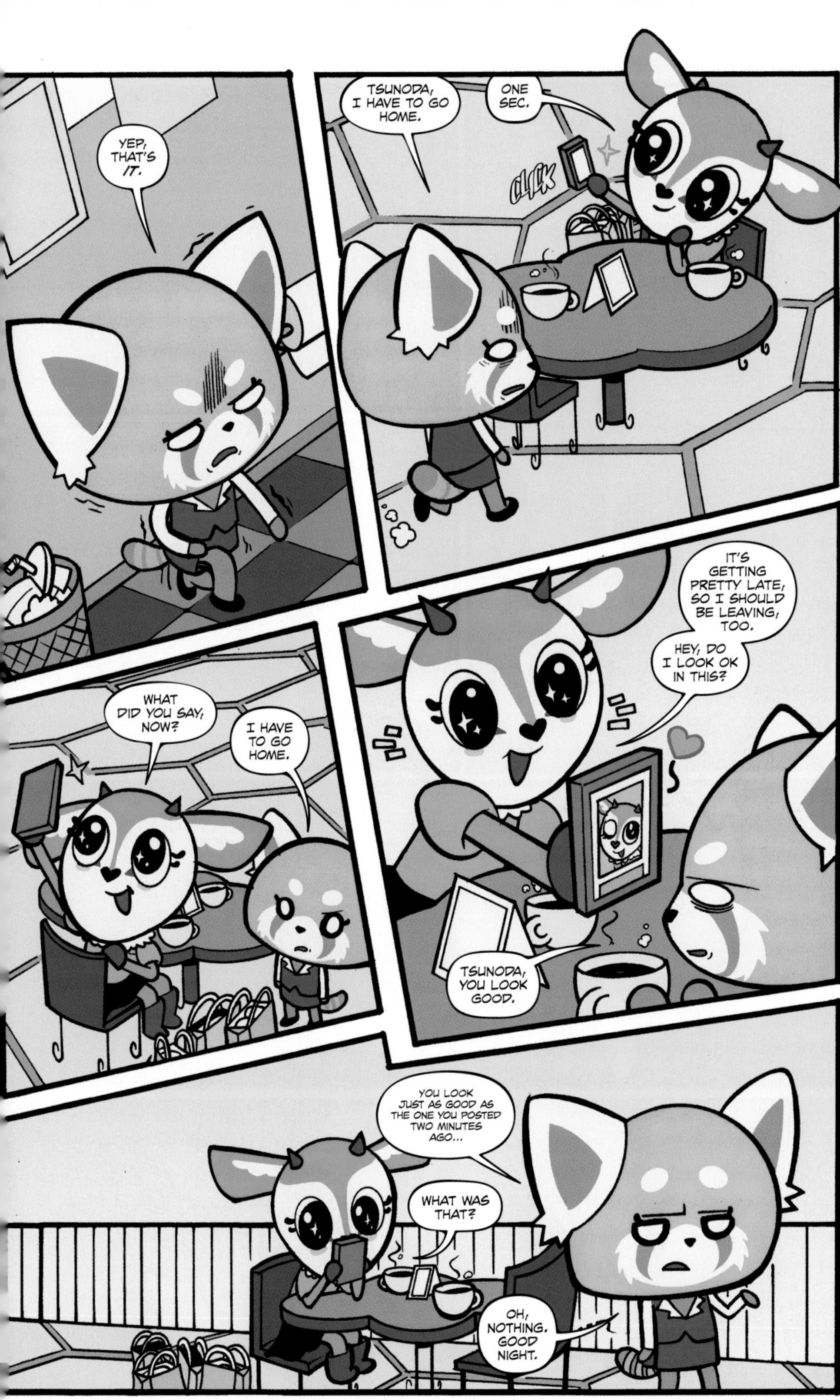
YEP, THAT'S IT.
TSUNODA, I HAVE TO GO HOME.
ONE SEC.
CLICK
WHAT DID YOU SAY, NOW?
I HAVE TO GO HOME.
IT'S GETTING PRETTY LATE, SO I SHOULD BE LEAVING, TOO.
HEY, DO I LOOK OK IN THIS?
TSUNODA, YOU LOOK GOOD.
YOU LOOK JUST AS GOOD AS THE ONE YOU POSTED TWO MINUTES AGO...
WHAT WAS THAT?
OH, NOTHING. GOOD NIGHT.

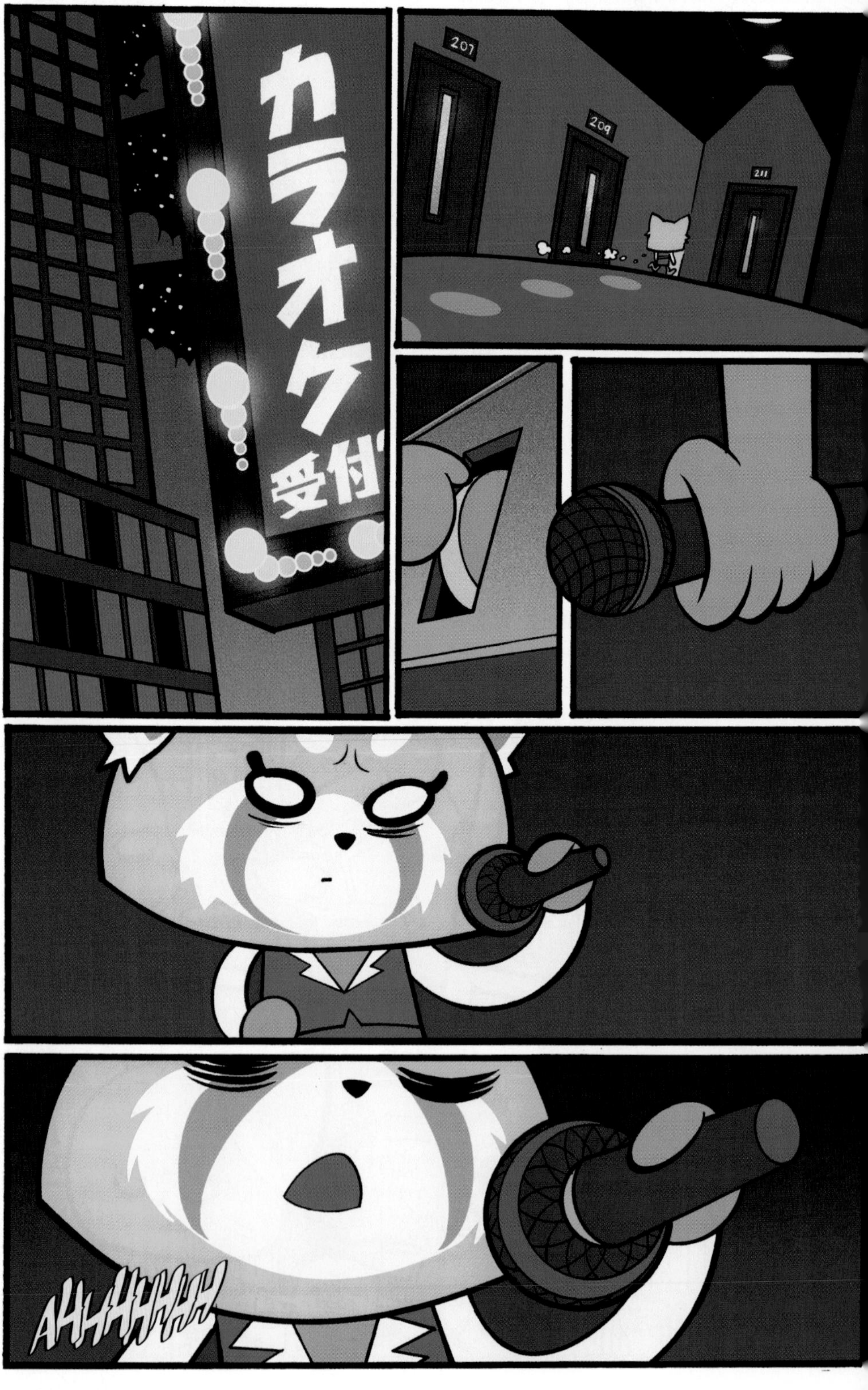
カラオケ
受付
207
209
211
AHHHHHH

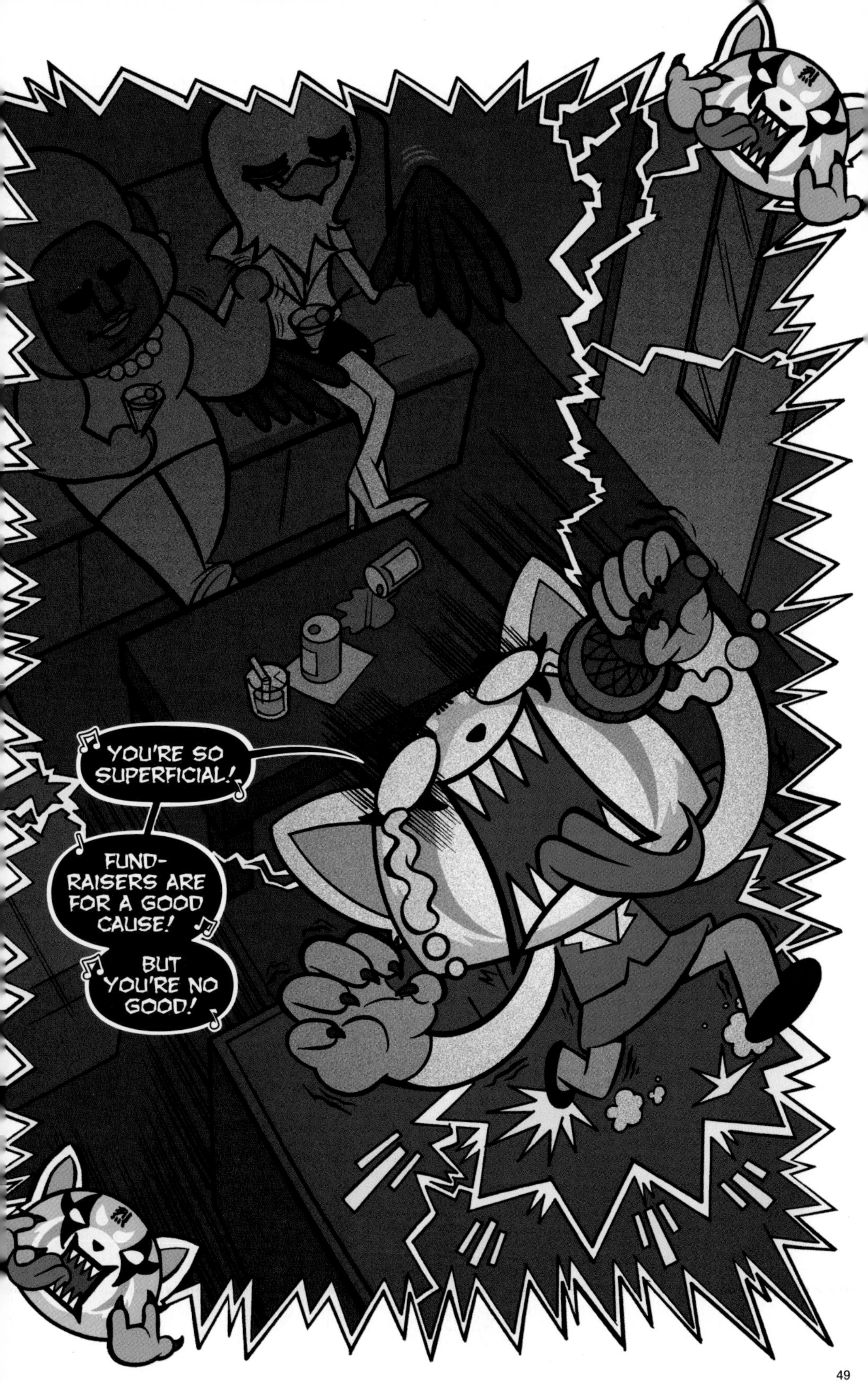
YOU'RE SO SUPERFICIAL!
FUND-RAISERS ARE FOR A GOOD CAUSE!
BUT YOU'RE NO GOOD!

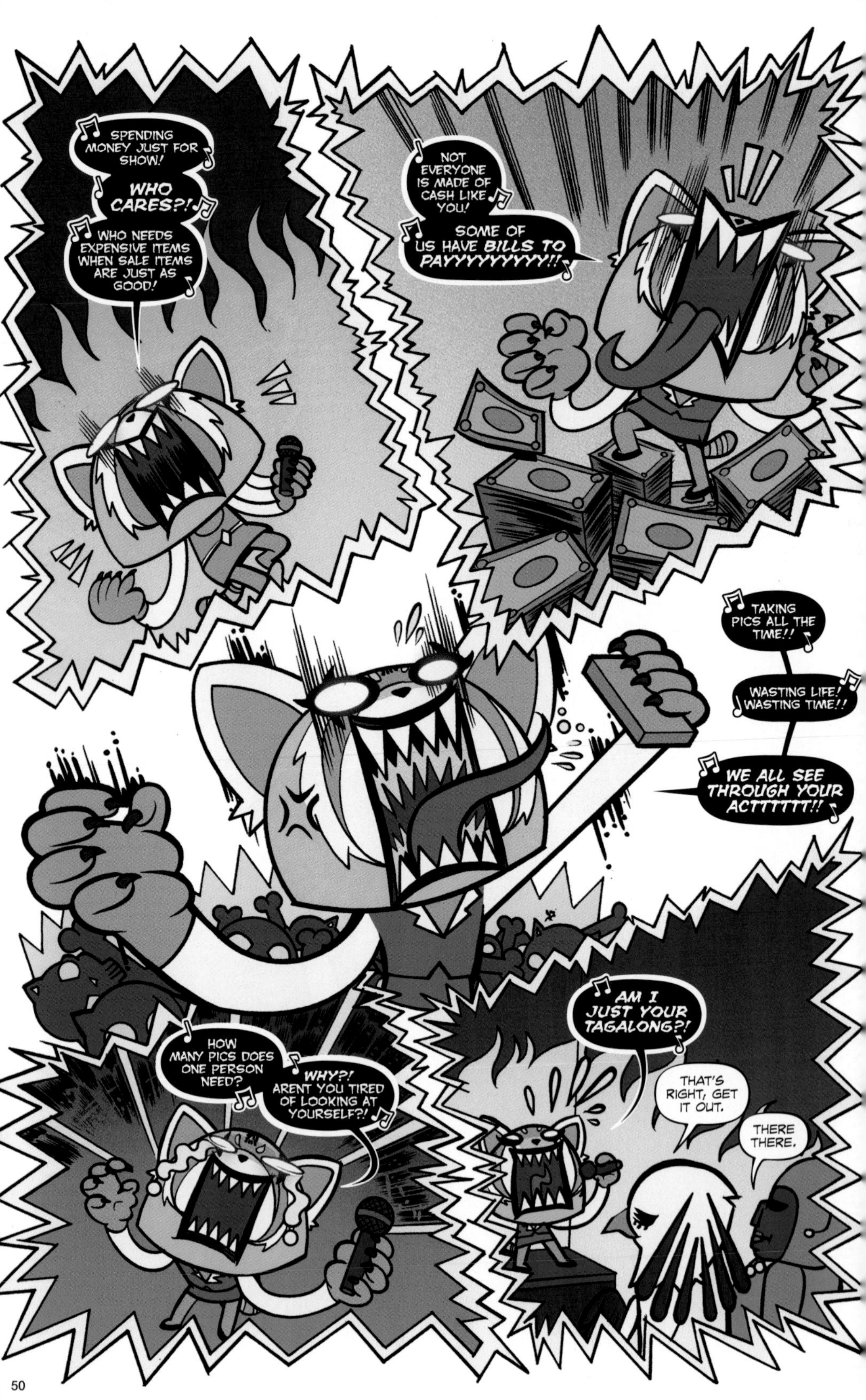

SPENDING MONEY JUST FOR SHOW!
WHO CARES?!
WHO NEEDS EXPENSIVE ITEMS WHEN SALE ITEMS ARE JUST AS GOOD!
NOT EVERYONE IS MADE OF CASH LIKE YOU!
SOME OF US HAVE BILLS TO PAYYYYYYYYY!!
TAKING PICS ALL THE TIME!!
WASTING LIFE! WASTING TIME!!
WE ALL SEE THROUGH YOUR ACTTTTTT!!
HOW MANY PICS DOES ONE PERSON NEED?
WHY?! ARENT YOU TIRED OF LOOKING AT YOURSELF?!
AM I JUST YOUR TAGALONG?!
THAT'S RIGHT, GET IT OUT.
THERE THERE.

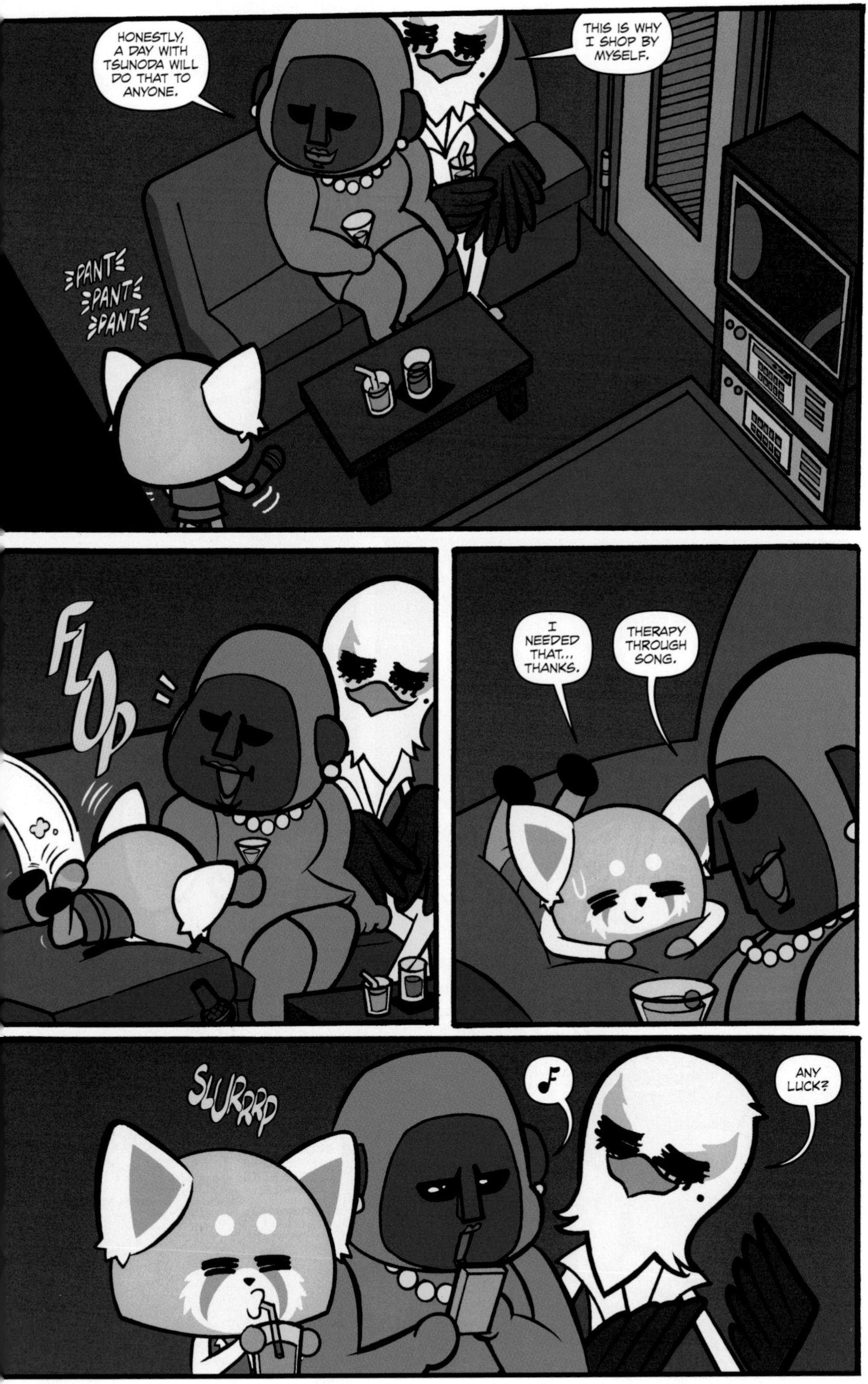
HONESTLY, A DAY WITH TSUNODA WILL DO THAT TO ANYONE.
THIS IS WHY I SHOP BY MYSELF.
PANT PANT PANT
FLOP
I NEEDED THAT... THANKS.
THERAPY THROUGH SONG.
SLURRRP
ANY LUCK?

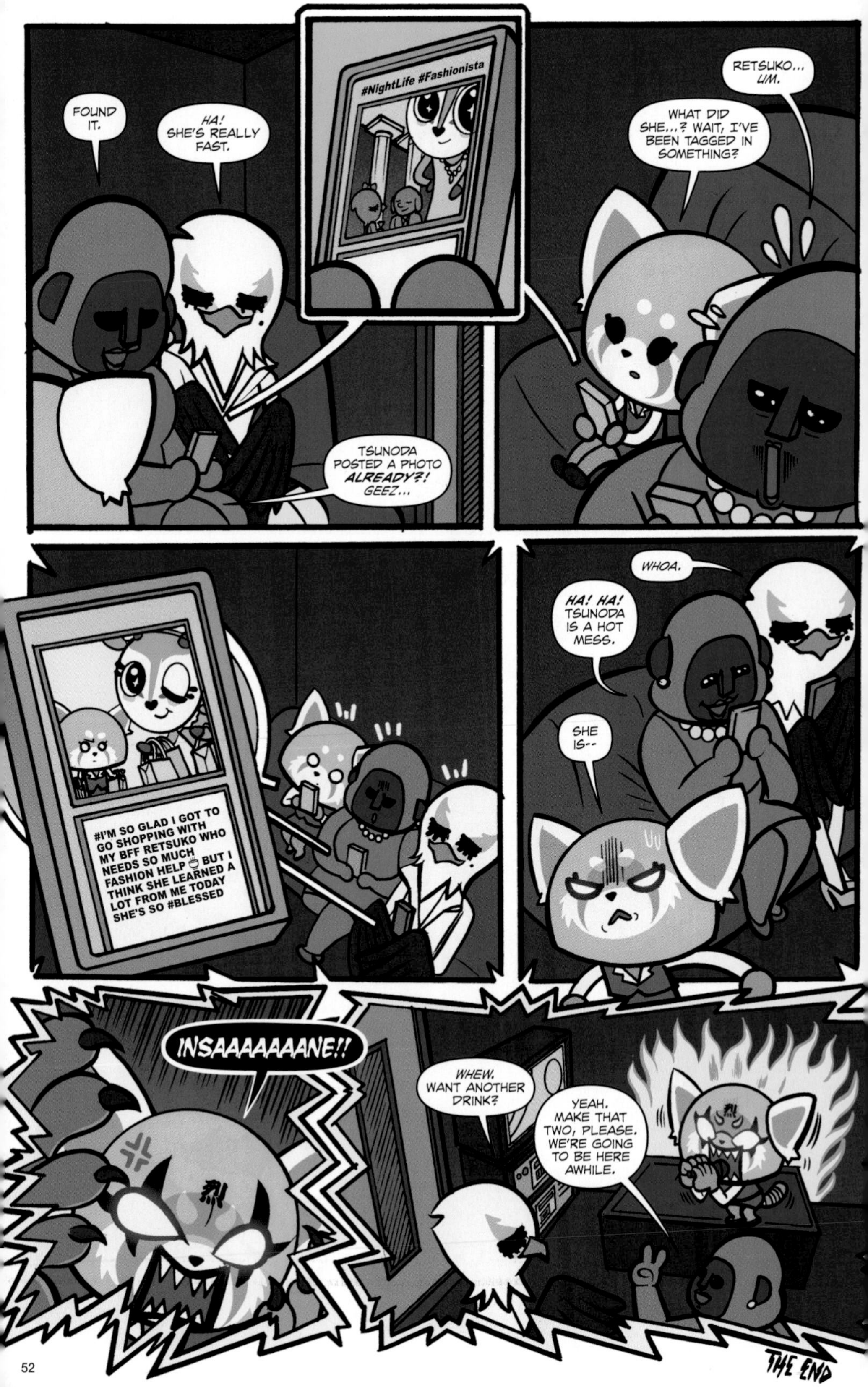
FOUND IT.
HA! SHE'S REALLY FAST.
#NightLife #Fashionista
TSUNODA POSTED A PHOTO ALREADY?! GEEZ...
RETSUKO... UM.
WHAT DID SHE...? WAIT, I'VE BEEN TAGGED IN SOMETHING?
#I'M SO GLAD I GOT TO GO SHOPPING WITH MY BFF RETSUKO WHO NEEDS SO MUCH FASHION HELP BUT I THINK SHE LEARNED A LOT FROM ME TODAY SHE'S SO #BLESSED
WHOA.
HA! HA! TSUNODA IS A HOT MESS.
SHE IS--
INSAAAAAAAANE!!
WHEW. WANT ANOTHER DRINK?
YEAH. MAKE THAT TWO, PLEASE. WE'RE GOING TO BE HERE AWHILE.
THE END

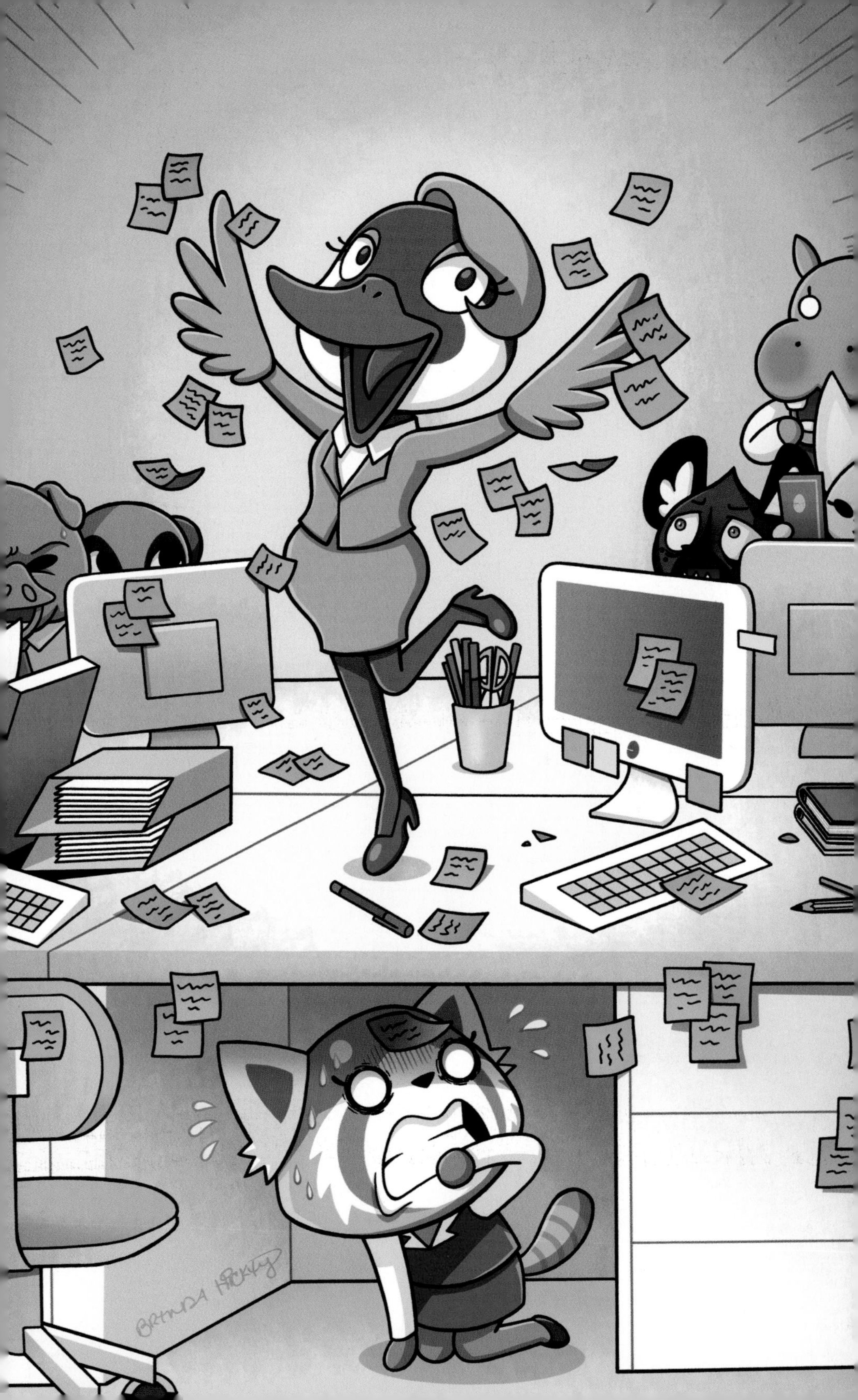

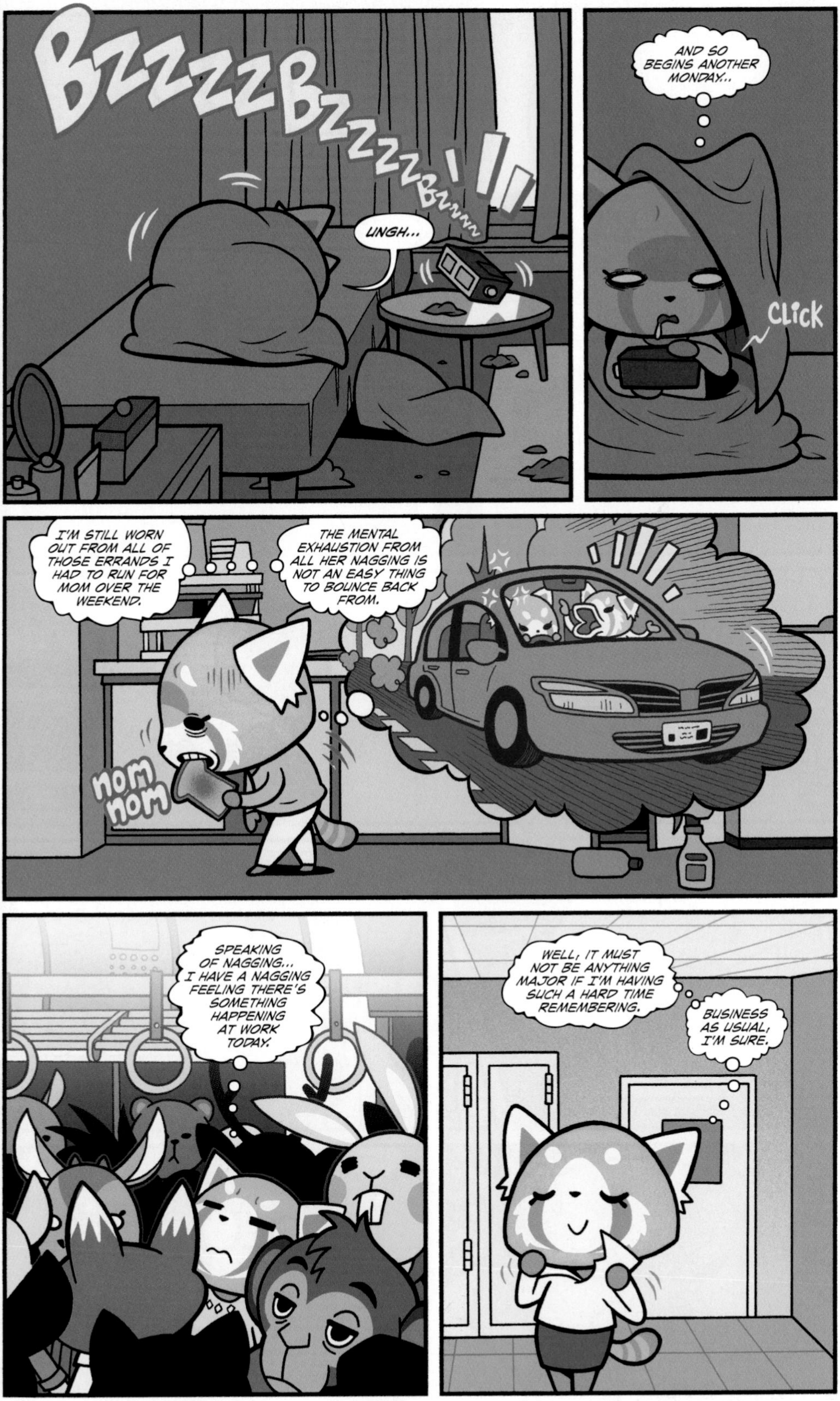
BZZZZZBZZZZZBZZZZ
UNGH...
AND SO BEGINS ANOTHER MONDAY...
CLICK
I'M STILL WORN OUT FROM ALL OF THOSE ERRANDS I HAD TO RUN FOR MOM OVER THE WEEKEND.
THE MENTAL EXHAUSTION FROM ALL HER NAGGING IS NOT AN EASY THING TO BOUNCE BACK FROM.
nom nom
SPEAKING OF NAGGING... I HAVE A NAGGING FEELING THERE'S SOMETHING HAPPENING AT WORK TODAY.
WELL, IT MUST NOT BE ANYTHING MAJOR IF I'M HAVING SUCH A HARD TIME REMEMBERING.
BUSINESS AS USUAL, I'M SURE.

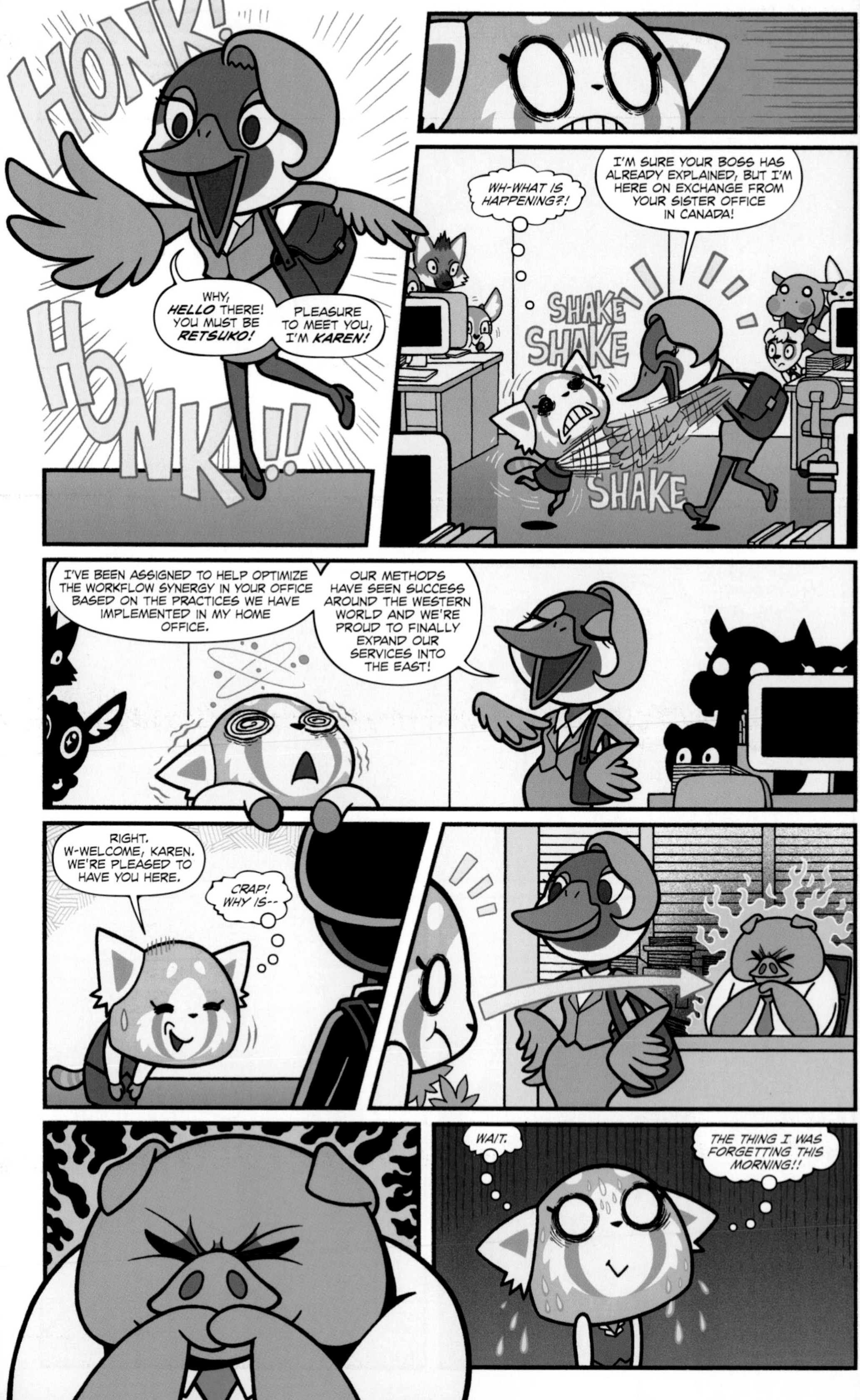
HONK!
HONK!!
WHY, HELLO THERE! YOU MUST BE RETSUKO!
PLEASURE TO MEET YOU, I'M KAREN!
WH-WHAT IS HAPPENING?!
I'M SURE YOUR BOSS HAS ALREADY EXPLAINED, BUT I'M HERE ON EXCHANGE FROM YOUR SISTER OFFICE IN CANADA!
SHAKE
SHAKE
SHAKE
I'VE BEEN ASSIGNED TO HELP OPTIMIZE THE WORKFLOW SYNERGY IN YOUR OFFICE BASED ON THE PRACTICES WE HAVE IMPLEMENTED IN MY HOME OFFICE.
OUR METHODS HAVE SEEN SUCCESS AROUND THE WESTERN WORLD AND WE'RE PROUD TO FINALLY EXPAND OUR SERVICES INTO THE EAST!
RIGHT. W-WELCOME, KAREN. WE'RE PLEASED TO HAVE YOU HERE.
CRAP! WHY IS--
WAIT.
THE THING I WAS FORGETTING THIS MORNING!!

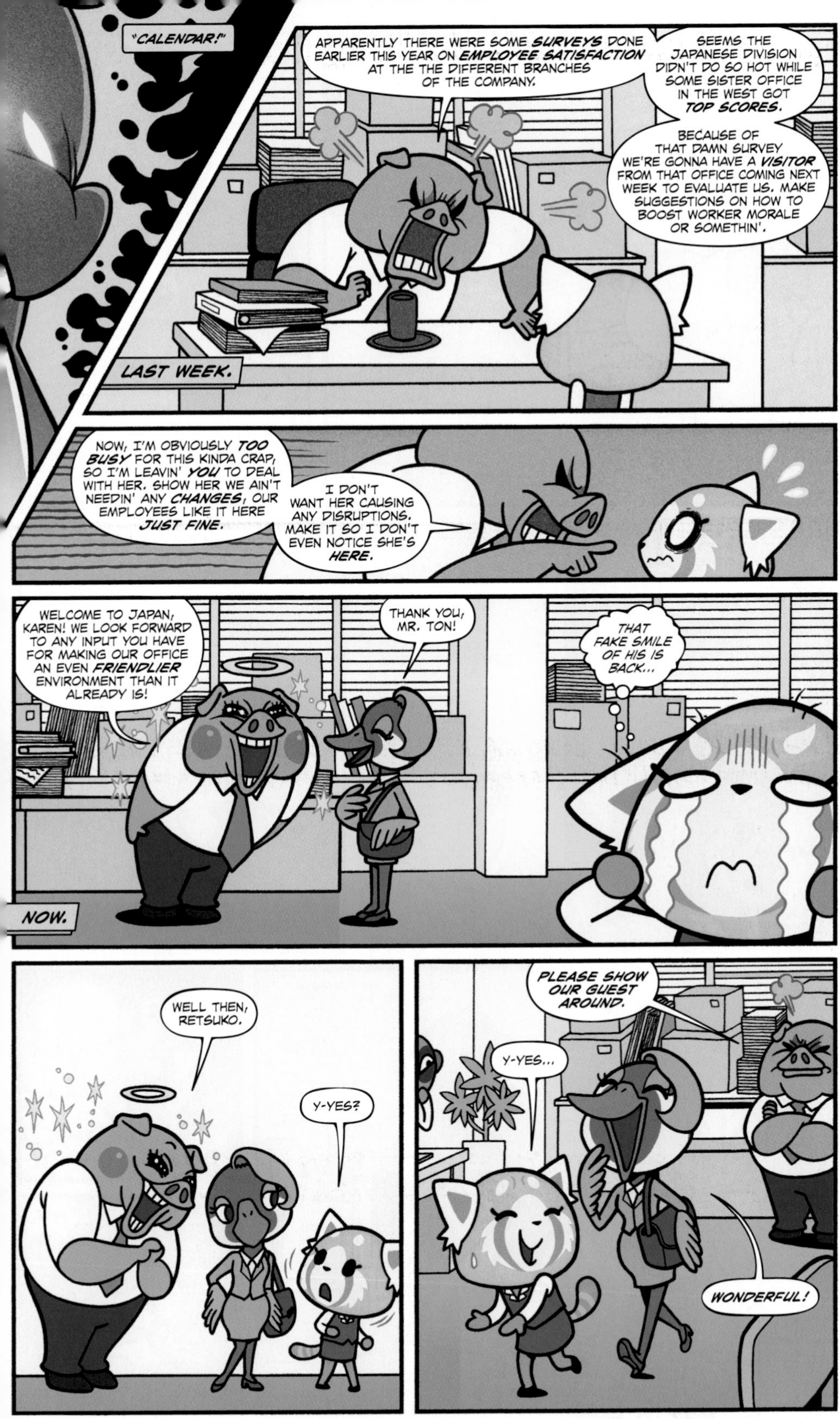
"CALENDAR!"
APPARENTLY THERE WERE SOME SURVEYS DONE EARLIER THIS YEAR ON EMPLOYEE SATISFACTION AT THE THE DIFFERENT BRANCHES OF THE COMPANY.
SEEMS THE JAPANESE DIVISION DIDN'T DO SO HOT WHILE SOME SISTER OFFICE IN THE WEST GOT TOP SCORES.
BECAUSE OF THAT DAMN SURVEY WE'RE GONNA HAVE A VISITOR FROM THAT OFFICE COMING NEXT WEEK TO EVALUATE US. MAKE SUGGESTIONS ON HOW TO BOOST WORKER MORALE OR SOMETHIN'.
LAST WEEK.
NOW, I'M OBVIOUSLY TOO BUSY FOR THIS KINDA CRAP, SO I'M LEAVIN' YOU TO DEAL WITH HER. SHOW HER WE AIN'T NEEDIN' ANY CHANGES; OUR EMPLOYEES LIKE IT HERE JUST FINE.
I DON'T WANT HER CAUSING ANY DISRUPTIONS. MAKE IT SO I DON'T EVEN NOTICE SHE'S HERE.
WELCOME TO JAPAN, KAREN! WE LOOK FORWARD TO ANY INPUT YOU HAVE FOR MAKING OUR OFFICE AN EVEN FRIENDLIER ENVIRONMENT THAN IT ALREADY IS!
THANK YOU, MR. TON!
THAT FAKE SMILE OF HIS IS BACK...
NOW.
WELL THEN, RETSUKO.
Y-YES?
PLEASE SHOW OUR GUEST AROUND.
Y-YES...
WONDERFUL!

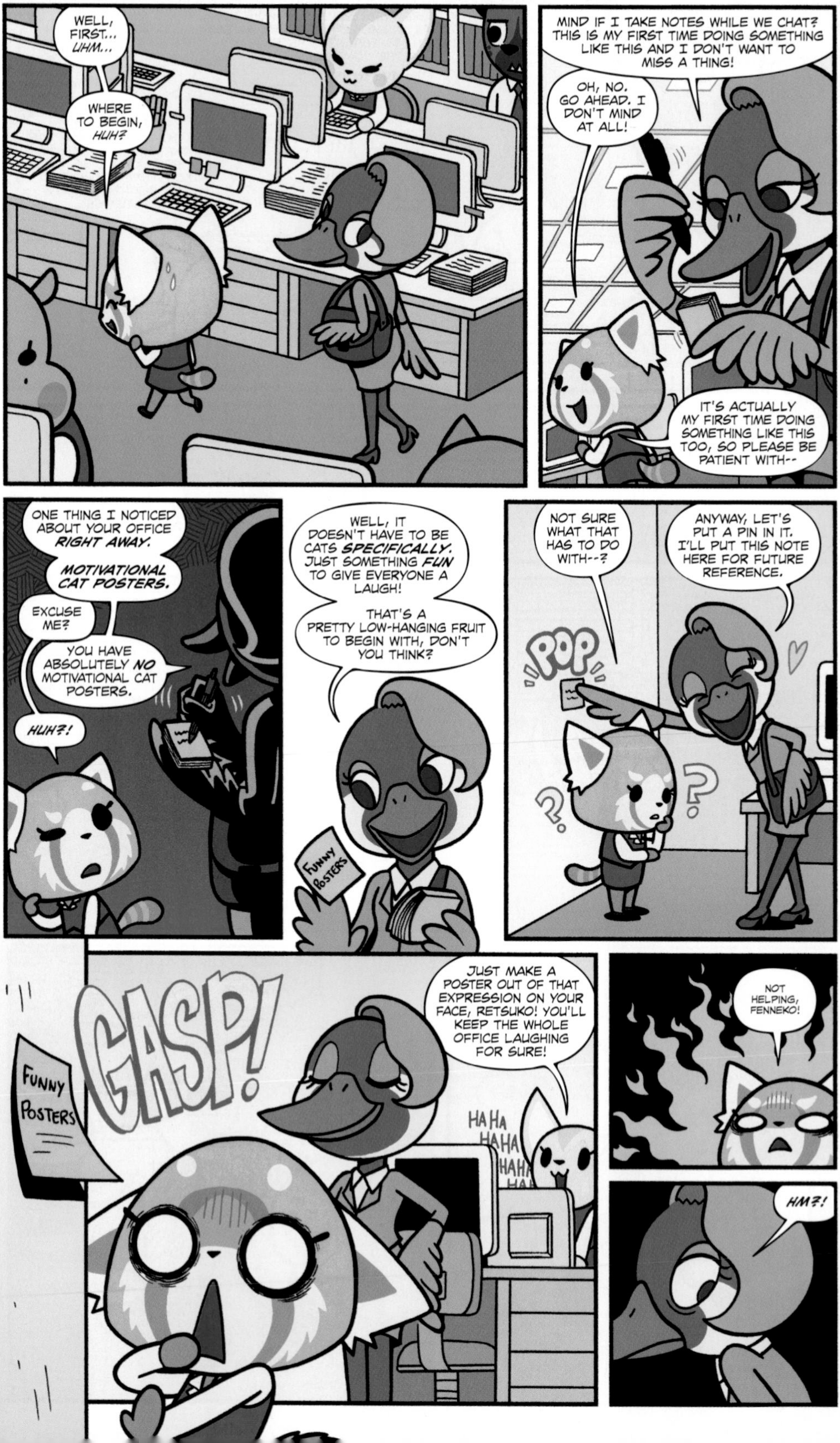
WELL, FIRST... UHM...
WHERE TO BEGIN, HUH?
MIND IF I TAKE NOTES WHILE WE CHAT? THIS IS MY FIRST TIME DOING SOMETHING LIKE THIS AND I DON'T WANT TO MISS A THING!
OH, NO. GO AHEAD. I DON'T MIND AT ALL!
IT'S ACTUALLY MY FIRST TIME DOING SOMETHING LIKE THIS TOO, SO PLEASE BE PATIENT WITH--
ONE THING I NOTICED ABOUT YOUR OFFICE RIGHT AWAY.
MOTIVATIONAL CAT POSTERS.
EXCUSE ME?
YOU HAVE ABSOLUTELY NO MOTIVATIONAL CAT POSTERS.
HUH?!
WELL, IT DOESN'T HAVE TO BE CATS SPECIFICALLY. JUST SOMETHING FUN TO GIVE EVERYONE A LAUGH!
THAT'S A PRETTY LOW-HANGING FRUIT TO BEGIN WITH, DON'T YOU THINK?
FUNNY POSTERS
NOT SURE WHAT THAT HAS TO DO WITH--?
ANYWAY, LET'S PUT A PIN IN IT. I'LL PUT THIS NOTE HERE FOR FUTURE REFERENCE.
POP
GASP!
FUNNY POSTERS
JUST MAKE A POSTER OUT OF THAT EXPRESSION ON YOUR FACE, RETSUKO! YOU'LL KEEP THE WHOLE OFFICE LAUGHING FOR SURE!
HA HA HA HA
NOT HELPING, FENNEKO!
HM?!

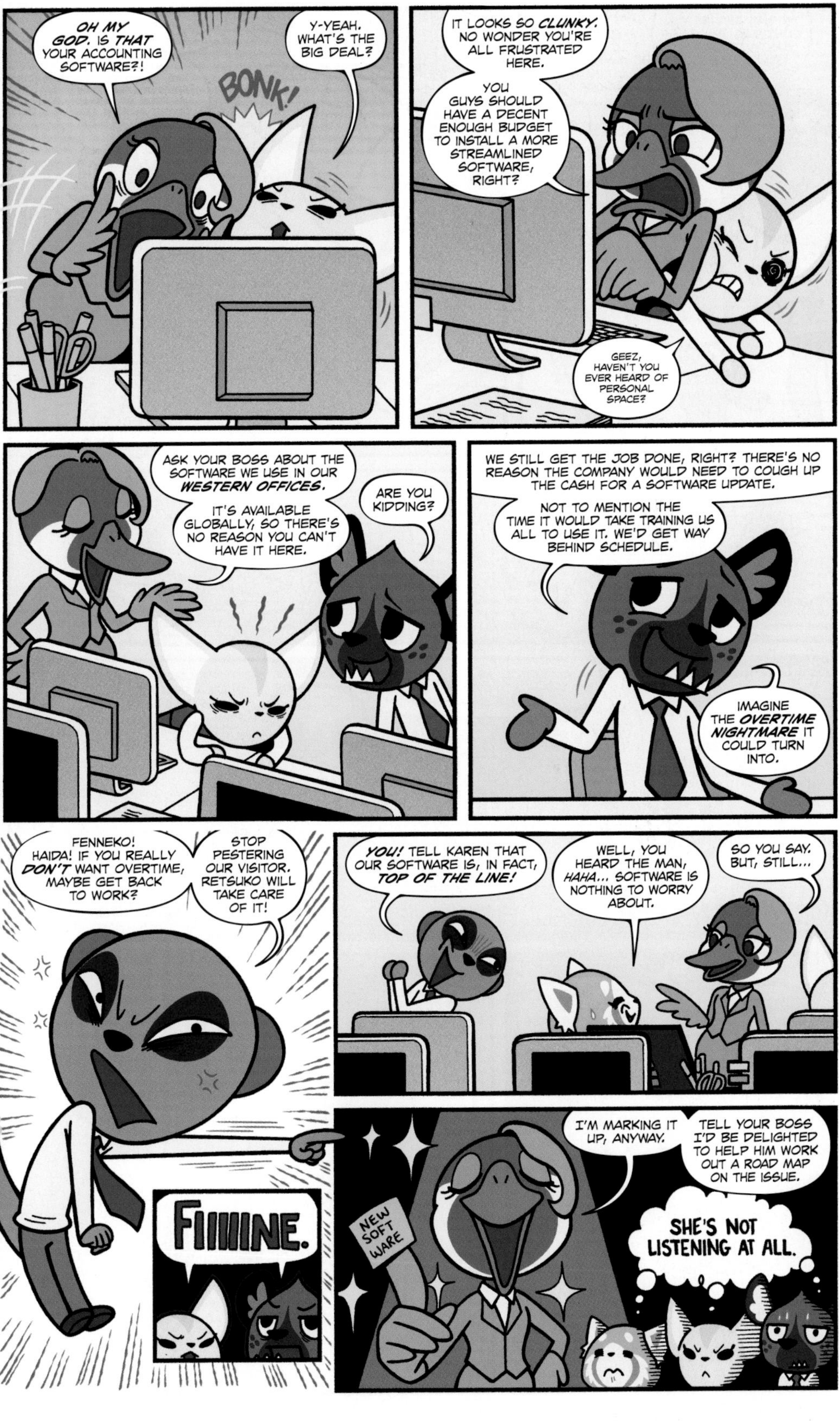

OH MY GOD. IS THAT YOUR ACCOUNTING SOFTWARE?!
Y-YEAH. WHAT'S THE BIG DEAL?
BONK!
IT LOOKS SO CLUNKY. NO WONDER YOU'RE ALL FRUSTRATED HERE.
YOU GUYS SHOULD HAVE A DECENT ENOUGH BUDGET TO INSTALL A MORE STREAMLINED SOFTWARE, RIGHT?
GEEZ, HAVEN'T YOU EVER HEARD OF PERSONAL SPACE?
ASK YOUR BOSS ABOUT THE SOFTWARE WE USE IN OUR WESTERN OFFICES.
IT'S AVAILABLE GLOBALLY, SO THERE'S NO REASON YOU CAN'T HAVE IT HERE.
ARE YOU KIDDING?
WE STILL GET THE JOB DONE, RIGHT? THERE'S NO REASON THE COMPANY WOULD NEED TO COUGH UP THE CASH FOR A SOFTWARE UPDATE.
NOT TO MENTION THE TIME IT WOULD TAKE TRAINING US ALL TO USE IT. WE'D GET WAY BEHIND SCHEDULE.
IMAGINE THE OVERTIME NIGHTMARE IT COULD TURN INTO.
FENNEKO! HAIDA! IF YOU REALLY DON'T WANT OVERTIME, MAYBE GET BACK TO WORK?
STOP PESTERING OUR VISITOR. RETSUKO WILL TAKE CARE OF IT!
FIIIIINE.
YOU! TELL KAREN THAT OUR SOFTWARE IS, IN FACT, TOP OF THE LINE!
WELL, YOU HEARD THE MAN, HAHA... SOFTWARE IS NOTHING TO WORRY ABOUT.
SO YOU SAY. BUT, STILL...
I'M MARKING IT UP, ANYWAY.
TELL YOUR BOSS I'D BE DELIGHTED TO HELP HIM WORK OUT A ROAD MAP ON THE ISSUE.
NEW SOFT WARE
SHE'S NOT LISTENING AT ALL.

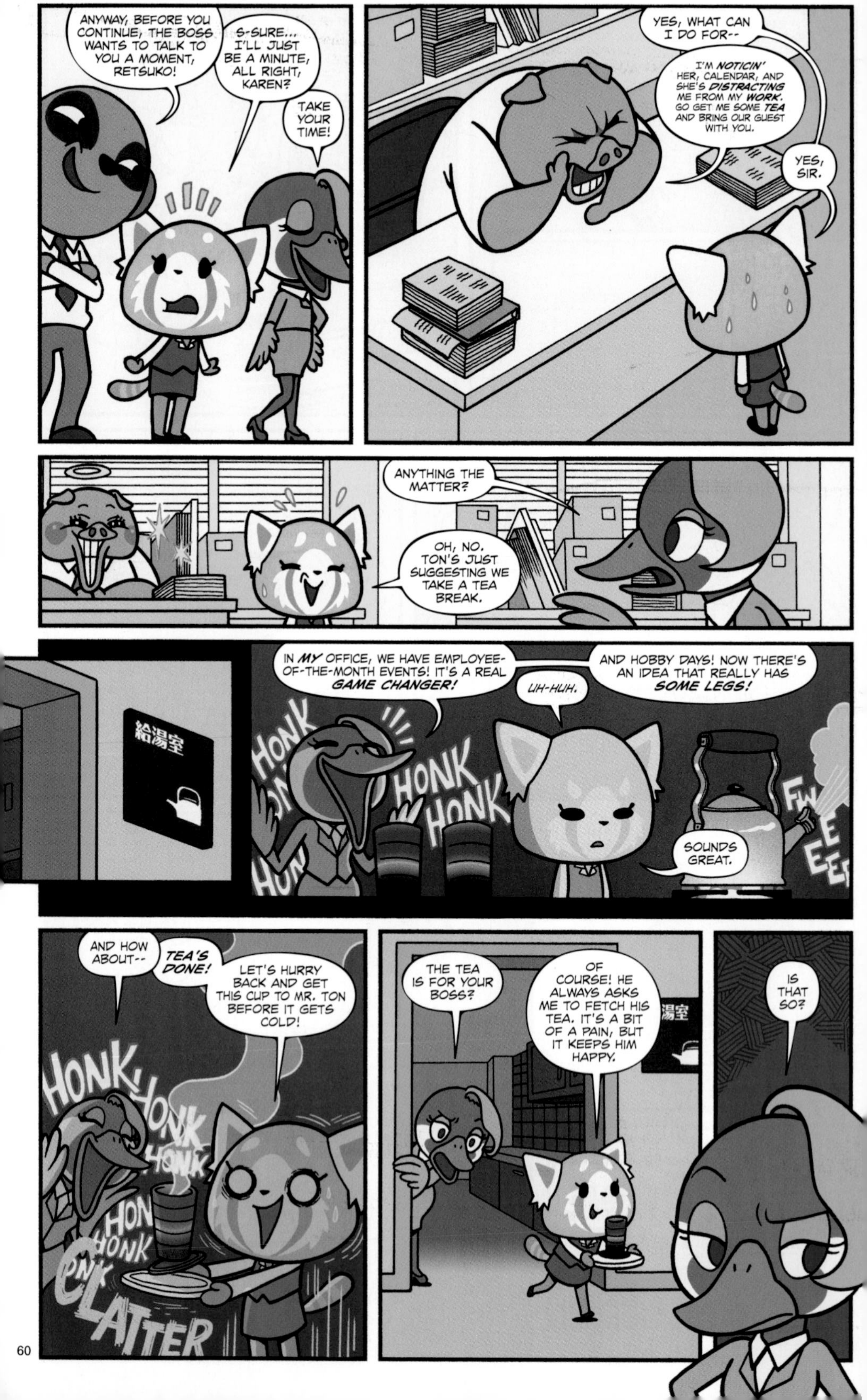
ANYWAY, BEFORE YOU CONTINUE, THE BOSS WANTS TO TALK TO YOU A MOMENT, RETSUKO!
S-SURE... I'LL JUST BE A MINUTE, ALL RIGHT, KAREN?
TAKE YOUR TIME!
YES, WHAT CAN I DO FOR--
I'M NOTICIN' HER, CALENDAR, AND SHE'S DISTRACTING ME FROM MY WORK. GO GET ME SOME TEA AND BRING OUR GUEST WITH YOU.
YES, SIR.
ANYTHING THE MATTER?
OH, NO. TON'S JUST SUGGESTING WE TAKE A TEA BREAK.
給湯室
IN MY OFFICE, WE HAVE EMPLOYEE-OF-THE-MONTH EVENTS! IT'S A REAL GAME CHANGER!
UH-HUH.
AND HOBBY DAYS! NOW THERE'S AN IDEA THAT REALLY HAS SOME LEGS!
HONK HONK HONK
SOUNDS GREAT.
FWEEE
AND HOW ABOUT--
TEA'S DONE!
LET'S HURRY BACK AND GET THIS CUP TO MR. TON BEFORE IT GETS COLD!
HONK HONK HONK HONK
CLATTER
THE TEA IS FOR YOUR BOSS?
OF COURSE! HE ALWAYS ASKS ME TO FETCH HIS TEA. IT'S A BIT OF A PAIN, BUT IT KEEPS HIM HAPPY.
IS THAT SO?

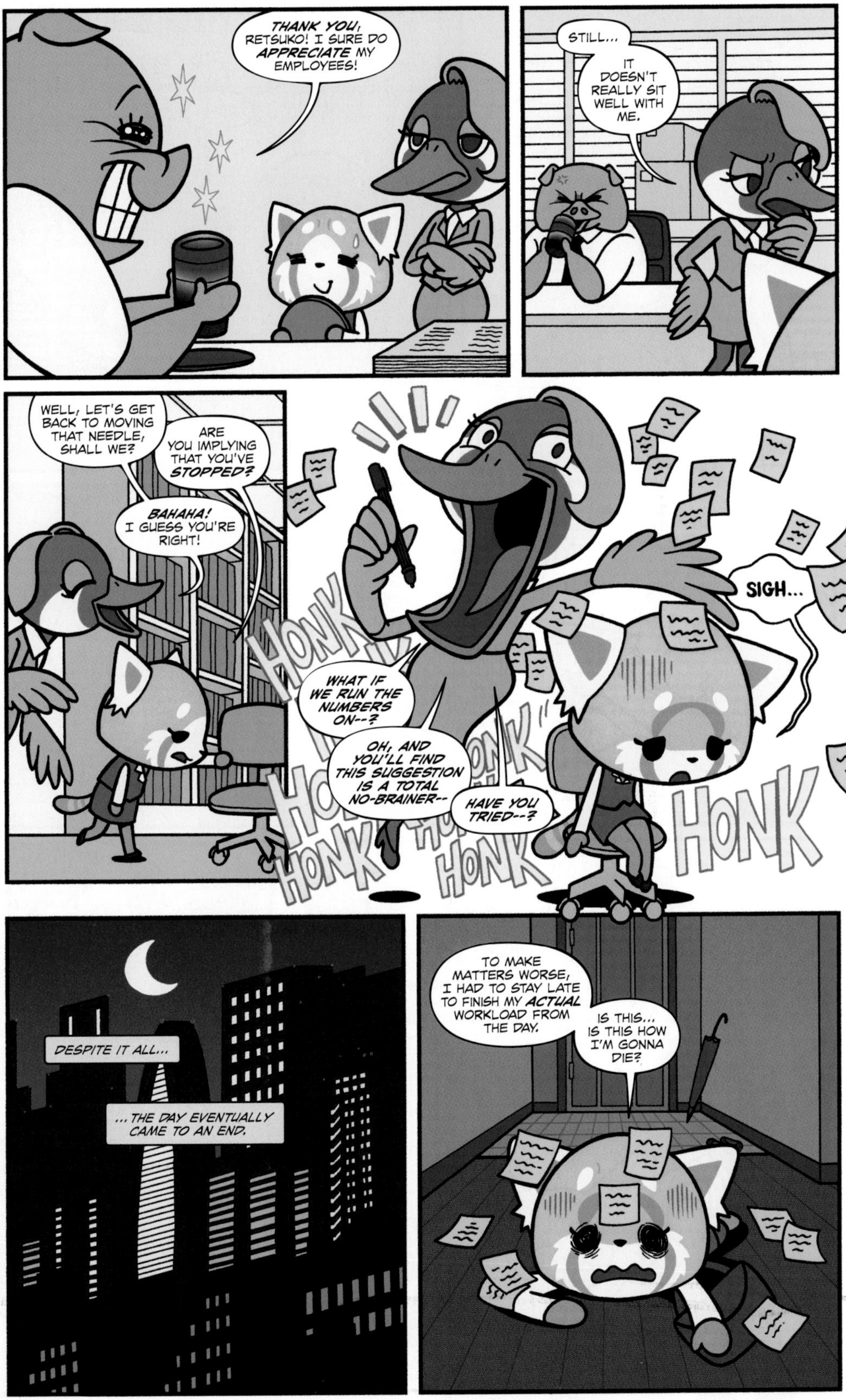
THANK YOU, RETSUKO! I SURE DO APPRECIATE MY EMPLOYEES!
STILL...
IT DOESN'T REALLY SIT WELL WITH ME.
WELL, LET'S GET BACK TO MOVING THAT NEEDLE, SHALL WE?
ARE YOU IMPLYING THAT YOU'VE STOPPED?
BAHAHA! I GUESS YOU'RE RIGHT!
HONK
WHAT IF WE RUN THE NUMBERS ON--?
OH, AND YOU'LL FIND THIS SUGGESTION IS A TOTAL NO-BRAINER--
HAVE YOU TRIED--?
HONK HONK HONK
SIGH...
HONK
DESPITE IT ALL...
...THE DAY EVENTUALLY CAME TO AN END.
TO MAKE MATTERS WORSE, I HAD TO STAY LATE TO FINISH MY ACTUAL WORKLOAD FROM THE DAY.
IS THIS... IS THIS HOW I'M GONNA DIE?

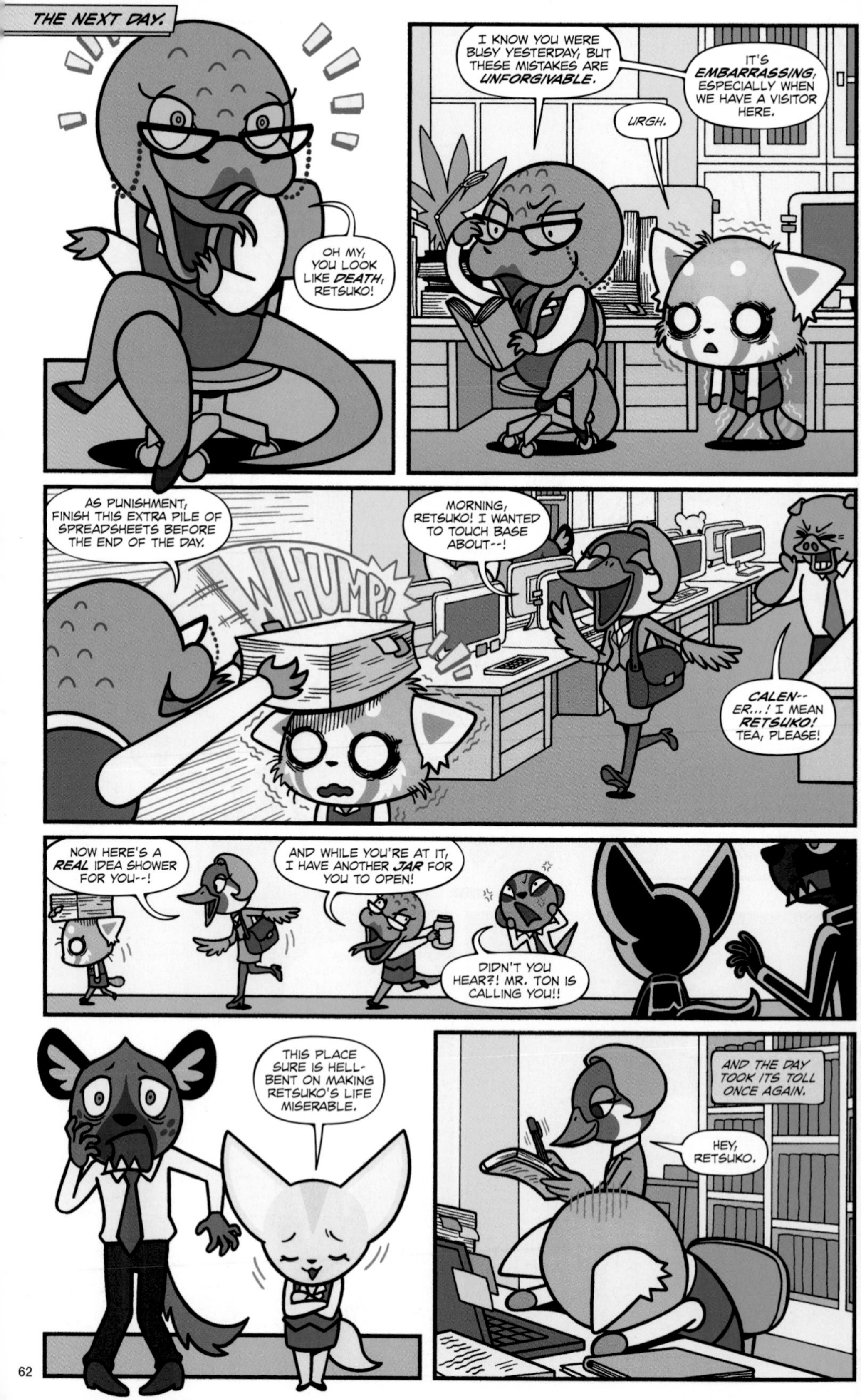
THE NEXT DAY.
OH MY, YOU LOOK LIKE DEATH, RETSUKO!
I KNOW YOU WERE BUSY YESTERDAY, BUT THESE MISTAKES ARE UNFORGIVABLE.
URGH.
IT'S EMBARRASSING, ESPECIALLY WHEN WE HAVE A VISITOR HERE.
AS PUNISHMENT, FINISH THIS EXTRA PILE OF SPREADSHEETS BEFORE THE END OF THE DAY.
WHUMP!
MORNING, RETSUKO! I WANTED TO TOUCH BASE ABOUT--!
CALEN-- ER...! I MEAN RETSUKO! TEA, PLEASE!
NOW HERE'S A REAL IDEA SHOWER FOR YOU--!
AND WHILE YOU'RE AT IT, I HAVE ANOTHER JAR FOR YOU TO OPEN!
DIDN'T YOU HEAR?! MR. TON IS CALLING YOU!!
THIS PLACE SURE IS HELL-BENT ON MAKING RETSUKO'S LIFE MISERABLE.
AND THE DAY TOOK ITS TOLL ONCE AGAIN.
HEY, RETSUKO.

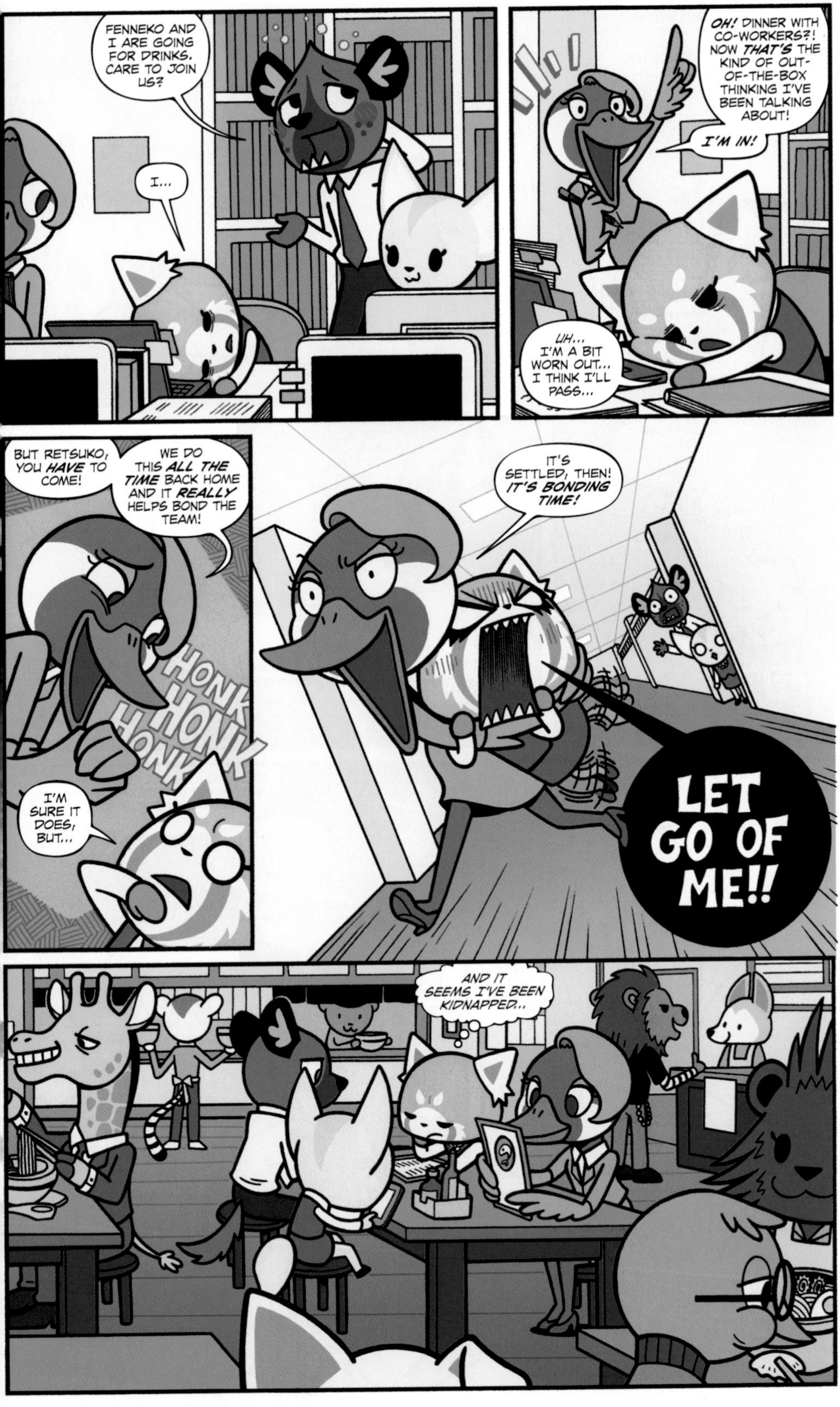
FENNEKO AND I ARE GOING FOR DRINKS. CARE TO JOIN US?
I...
OH! DINNER WITH CO-WORKERS?! NOW THAT'S THE KIND OF OUT-OF-THE-BOX THINKING I'VE BEEN TALKING ABOUT!
I'M IN!
UH... I'M A BIT WORN OUT... I THINK I'LL PASS...
BUT RETSUKO, YOU HAVE TO COME!
WE DO THIS ALL THE TIME BACK HOME AND IT REALLY HELPS BOND THE TEAM!
HONK HONK HONK
I'M SURE IT DOES, BUT...
IT'S SETTLED, THEN! IT'S BONDING TIME!
LET GO OF ME!!
AND IT SEEMS I'VE BEEN KIDNAPPED...

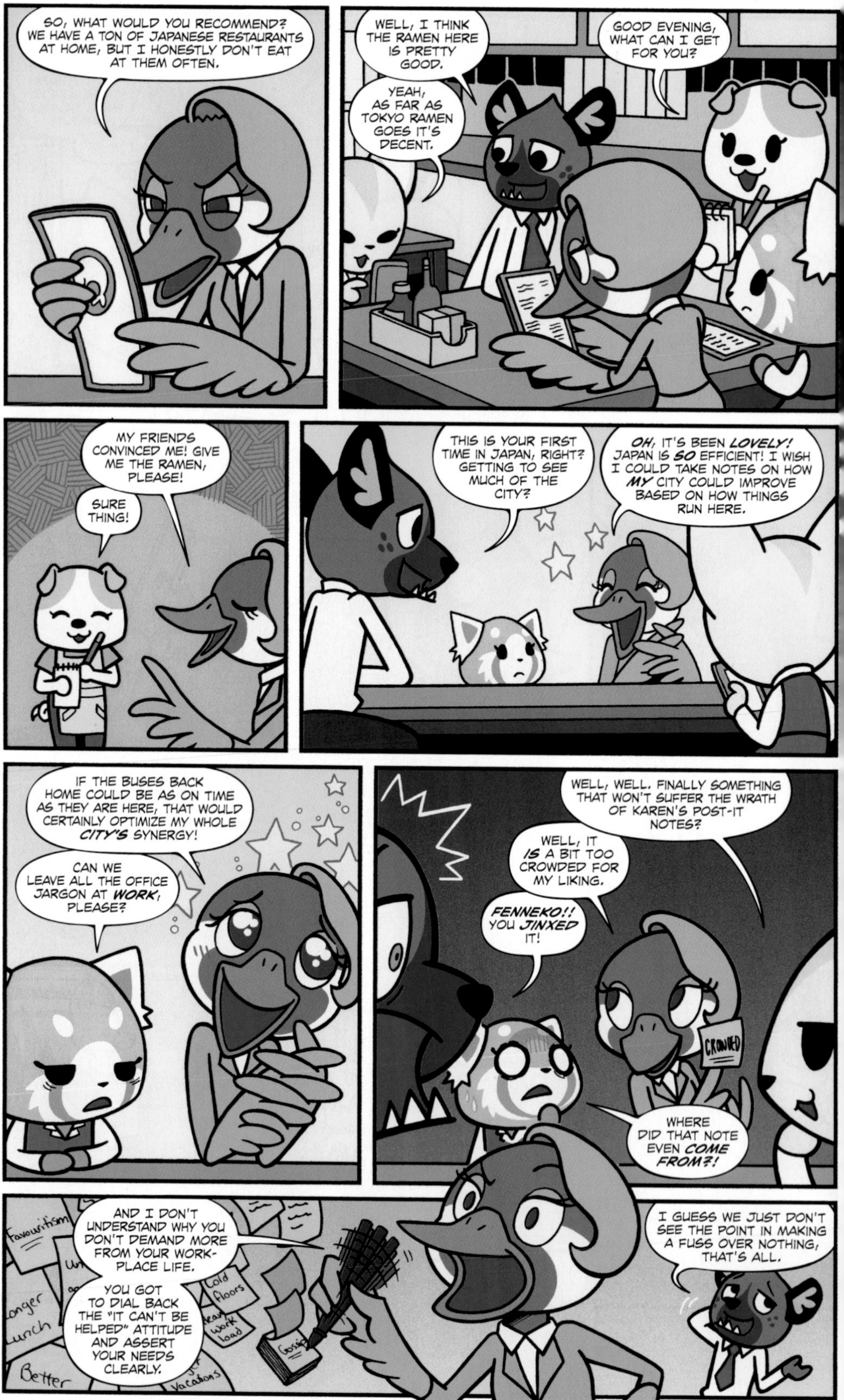
SO, WHAT WOULD YOU RECOMMEND? WE HAVE A TON OF JAPANESE RESTAURANTS AT HOME, BUT I HONESTLY DON'T EAT AT THEM OFTEN.
WELL, I THINK THE RAMEN HERE IS PRETTY GOOD.
YEAH, AS FAR AS TOKYO RAMEN GOES IT'S DECENT.
GOOD EVENING, WHAT CAN I GET FOR YOU?
MY FRIENDS CONVINCED ME! GIVE ME THE RAMEN, PLEASE!
SURE THING!
THIS IS YOUR FIRST TIME IN JAPAN, RIGHT? GETTING TO SEE MUCH OF THE CITY?
OH, IT'S BEEN LOVELY! JAPAN IS SO EFFICIENT! I WISH I COULD TAKE NOTES ON HOW MY CITY COULD IMPROVE BASED ON HOW THINGS RUN HERE.
IF THE BUSES BACK HOME COULD BE AS ON TIME AS THEY ARE HERE, THAT WOULD CERTAINLY OPTIMIZE MY WHOLE CITY'S SYNERGY!
CAN WE LEAVE ALL THE OFFICE JARGON AT WORK, PLEASE?
WELL, WELL. FINALLY SOMETHING THAT WON'T SUFFER THE WRATH OF KAREN'S POST-IT NOTES?
WELL, IT IS A BIT TOO CROWDED FOR MY LIKING.
FENNEKO!! YOU JINXED IT!
CROWDED
WHERE DID THAT NOTE EVEN COME FROM?!
AND I DON'T UNDERSTAND WHY YOU DON'T DEMAND MORE FROM YOUR WORK-PLACE LIFE.
YOU GOT TO DIAL BACK THE "IT CAN'T BE HELPED" ATTITUDE AND ASSERT YOUR NEEDS CLEARLY.
I GUESS WE JUST DON'T SEE THE POINT IN MAKING A FUSS OVER NOTHING, THAT'S ALL.
Favouritism
Longer Lunch
Better
Cold floors
Vacations
Gossip

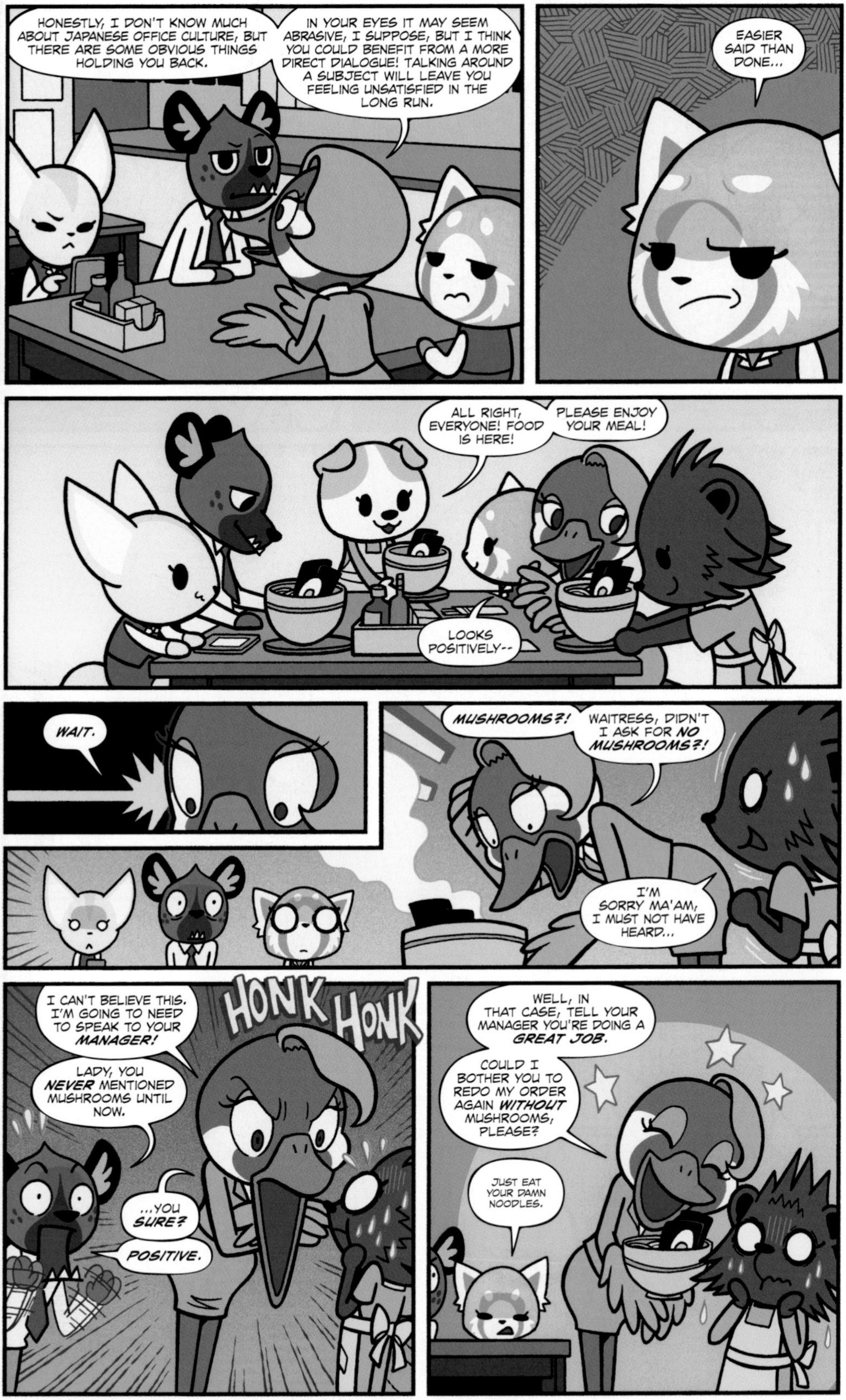
HONESTLY, I DON'T KNOW MUCH ABOUT JAPANESE OFFICE CULTURE, BUT THERE ARE SOME OBVIOUS THINGS HOLDING YOU BACK.
IN YOUR EYES IT MAY SEEM ABRASIVE, I SUPPOSE, BUT I THINK YOU COULD BENEFIT FROM A MORE DIRECT DIALOGUE! TALKING AROUND A SUBJECT WILL LEAVE YOU FEELING UNSATISFIED IN THE LONG RUN.
EASIER SAID THAN DONE...
ALL RIGHT, EVERYONE! FOOD IS HERE!
PLEASE ENJOY YOUR MEAL!
LOOKS POSITIVELY--
WAIT.
MUSHROOMS?!
WAITRESS, DIDN'T I ASK FOR NO MUSHROOMS?!
I'M SORRY MA'AM, I MUST NOT HAVE HEARD...
I CAN'T BELIEVE THIS. I'M GOING TO NEED TO SPEAK TO YOUR MANAGER!
HONK HONK
LADY, YOU NEVER MENTIONED MUSHROOMS UNTIL NOW.
...YOU SURE?
POSITIVE.
WELL, IN THAT CASE, TELL YOUR MANAGER YOU'RE DOING A GREAT JOB.
COULD I BOTHER YOU TO REDO MY ORDER AGAIN WITHOUT MUSHROOMS, PLEASE?
JUST EAT YOUR DAMN NOODLES.

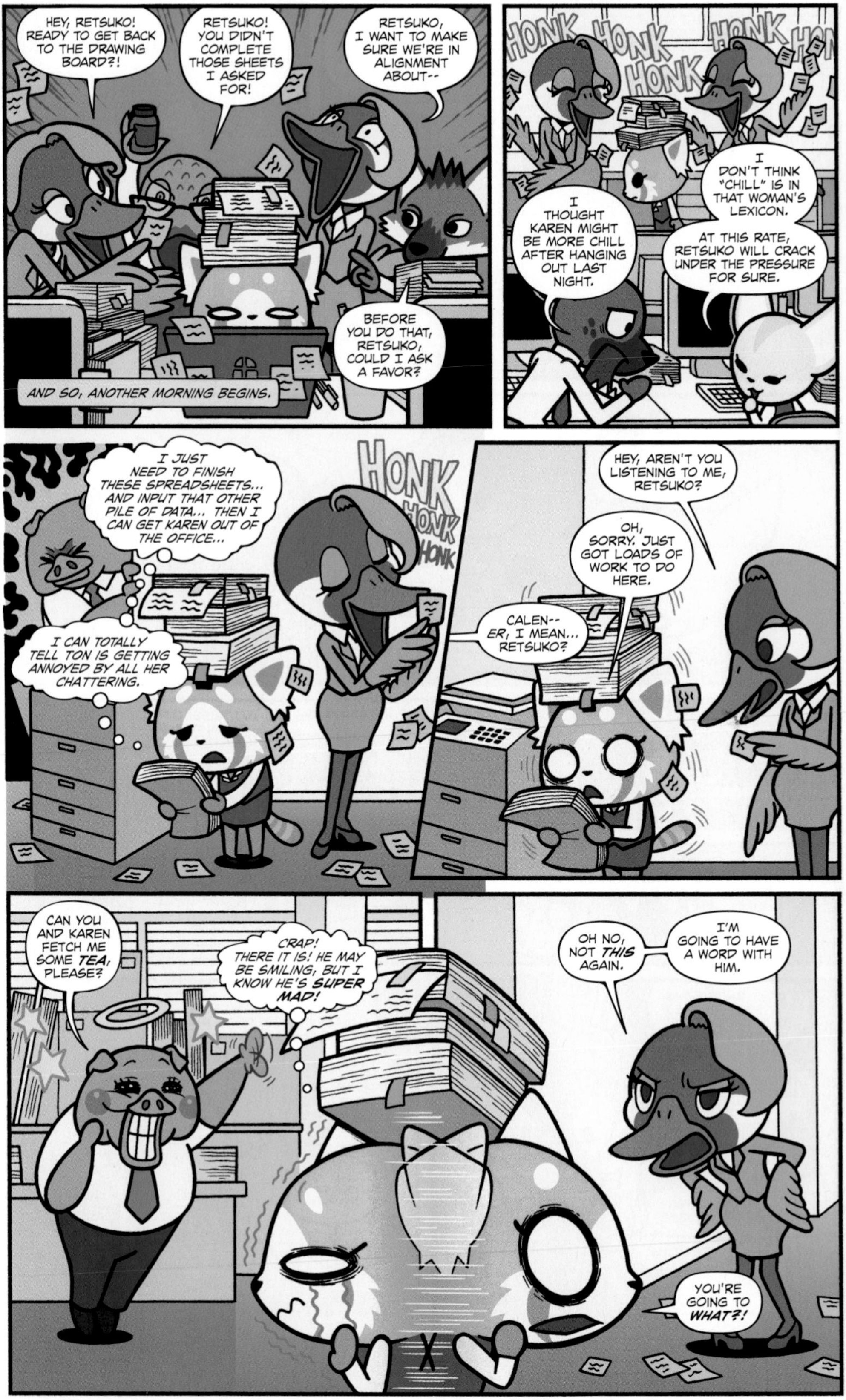
HEY, RETSUKO! READY TO GET BACK TO THE DRAWING BOARD?!
RETSUKO! YOU DIDN'T COMPLETE THOSE SHEETS I ASKED FOR!
RETSUKO, I WANT TO MAKE SURE WE'RE IN ALIGNMENT ABOUT--
BEFORE YOU DO THAT, RETSUKO, COULD I ASK A FAVOR?
AND SO, ANOTHER MORNING BEGINS.
HONK HONK HONK HONK HONK
I THOUGHT KAREN MIGHT BE MORE CHILL AFTER HANGING OUT LAST NIGHT.
I DON'T THINK "CHILL" IS IN THAT WOMAN'S LEXICON.
AT THIS RATE, RETSUKO WILL CRACK UNDER THE PRESSURE FOR SURE.
I JUST NEED TO FINISH THESE SPREADSHEETS... AND INPUT THAT OTHER PILE OF DATA... THEN I CAN GET KAREN OUT OF THE OFFICE...
I CAN TOTALLY TELL TON IS GETTING ANNOYED BY ALL HER CHATTERING.
HONK HONK HONK
HEY, AREN'T YOU LISTENING TO ME, RETSUKO?
OH, SORRY. JUST GOT LOADS OF WORK TO DO HERE.
CALEN-- ER, I MEAN... RETSUKO?
CAN YOU AND KAREN FETCH ME SOME TEA, PLEASE?
CRAP! THERE IT IS! HE MAY BE SMILING, BUT I KNOW HE'S SUPER MAD!
OH NO, NOT THIS AGAIN.
I'M GOING TO HAVE A WORD WITH HIM.
YOU'RE GOING TO WHAT?!

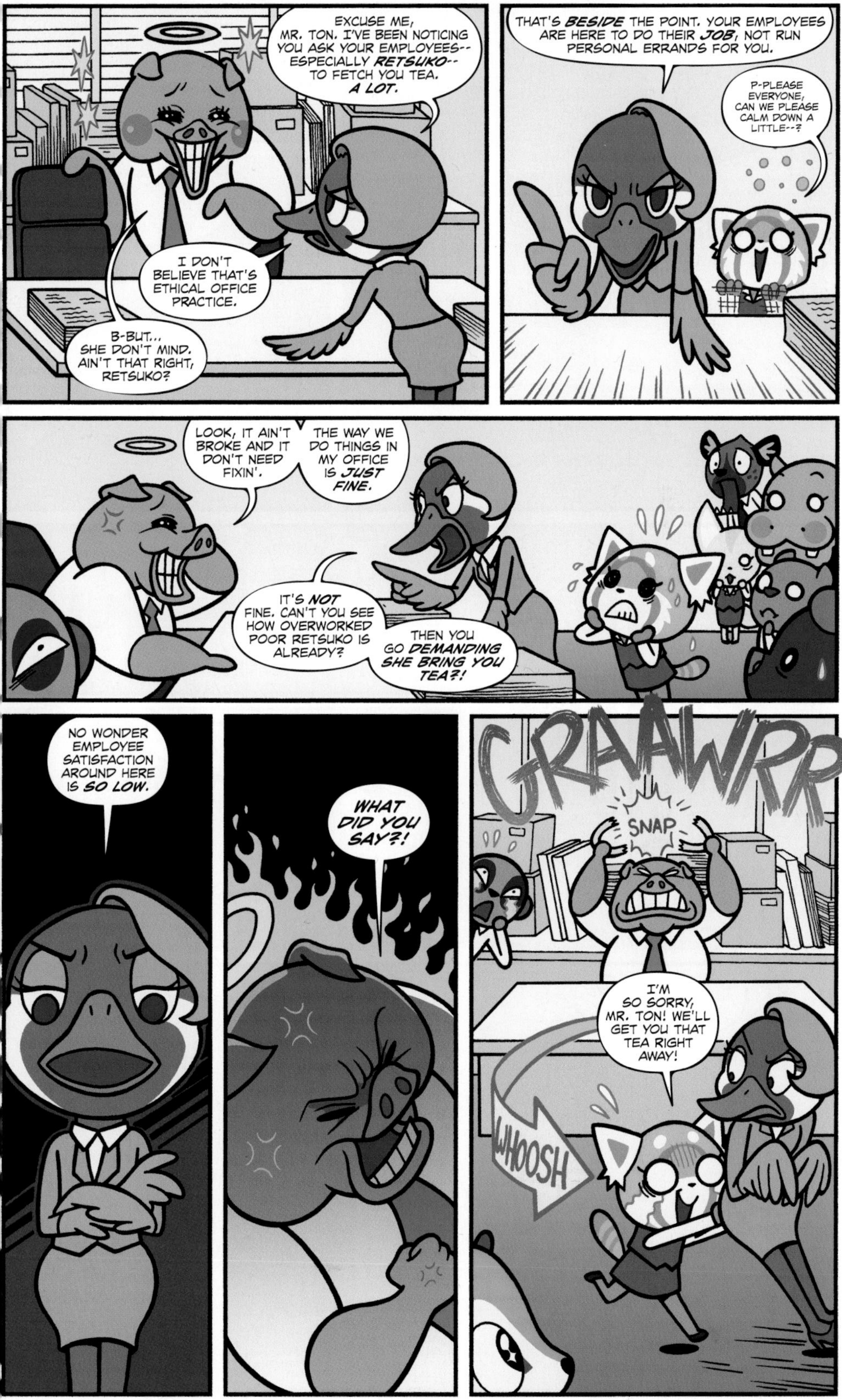
EXCUSE ME, MR. TON. I'VE BEEN NOTICING YOU ASK YOUR EMPLOYEES-- ESPECIALLY RETSUKO-- TO FETCH YOU TEA. A LOT.
I DON'T BELIEVE THAT'S ETHICAL OFFICE PRACTICE.
B-BUT... SHE DON'T MIND. AIN'T THAT RIGHT, RETSUKO?
THAT'S BESIDE THE POINT. YOUR EMPLOYEES ARE HERE TO DO THEIR JOB, NOT RUN PERSONAL ERRANDS FOR YOU.
P-PLEASE EVERYONE, CAN WE PLEASE CALM DOWN A LITTLE--?
LOOK, IT AIN'T BROKE AND IT DON'T NEED FIXIN'.
THE WAY WE DO THINGS IN MY OFFICE IS JUST FINE.
IT'S NOT FINE. CAN'T YOU SEE HOW OVERWORKED POOR RETSUKO IS ALREADY?
THEN YOU GO DEMANDING SHE BRING YOU TEA?!
NO WONDER EMPLOYEE SATISFACTION AROUND HERE IS SO LOW.
WHAT DID YOU SAY?!
GRAAWRR
SNAP
I'M SO SORRY, MR. TON! WE'LL GET YOU THAT TEA RIGHT AWAY!
WHOOSH

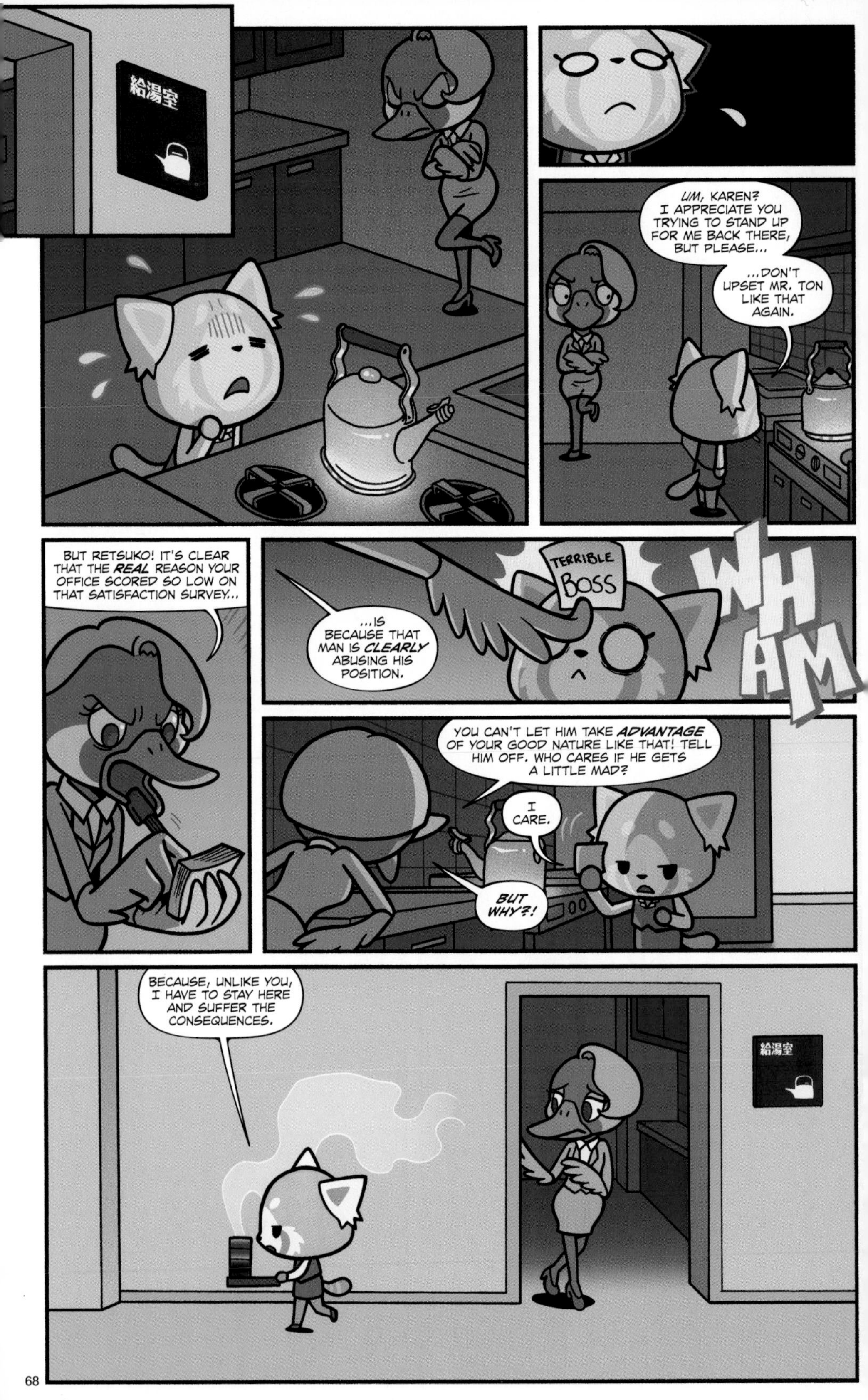
給湯室
UM, KAREN? I APPRECIATE YOU TRYING TO STAND UP FOR ME BACK THERE, BUT PLEASE...
...DON'T UPSET MR. TON LIKE THAT AGAIN.
BUT RETSUKO! IT'S CLEAR THAT THE REAL REASON YOUR OFFICE SCORED SO LOW ON THAT SATISFACTION SURVEY...
...IS BECAUSE THAT MAN IS CLEARLY ABUSING HIS POSITION.
TERRIBLE BOSS
WHAM
YOU CAN'T LET HIM TAKE ADVANTAGE OF YOUR GOOD NATURE LIKE THAT! TELL HIM OFF. WHO CARES IF HE GETS A LITTLE MAD?
I CARE.
BUT WHY?!
BECAUSE, UNLIKE YOU, I HAVE TO STAY HERE AND SUFFER THE CONSEQUENCES.
給湯室

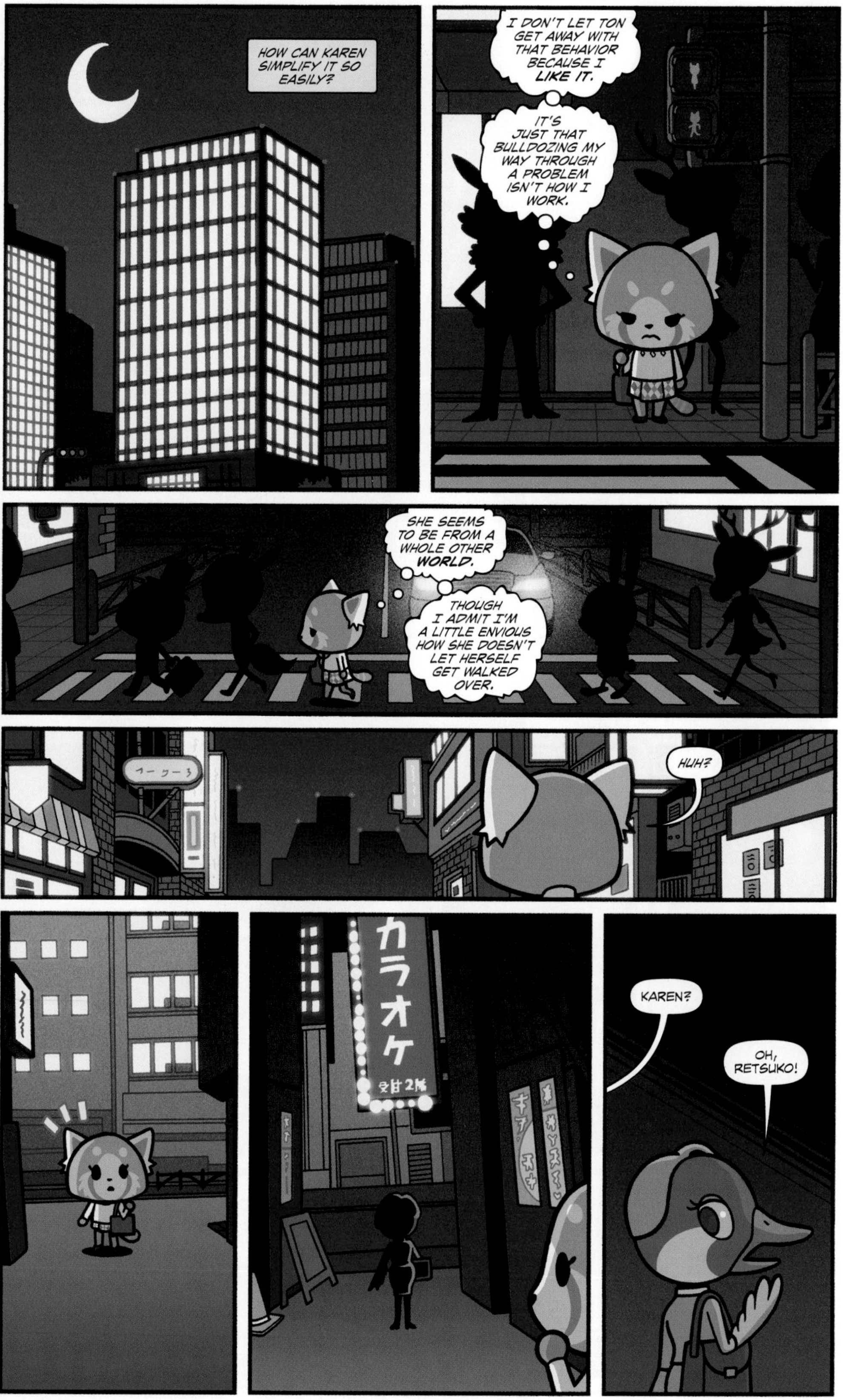
HOW CAN KAREN SIMPLIFY IT SO EASILY?
I DON'T LET TON GET AWAY WITH THAT BEHAVIOR BECAUSE I LIKE IT.
IT'S JUST THAT BULLDOZING MY WAY THROUGH A PROBLEM ISN'T HOW I WORK.
SHE SEEMS TO BE FROM A WHOLE OTHER WORLD.
THOUGH I ADMIT I'M A LITTLE ENVIOUS HOW SHE DOESN'T LET HERSELF GET WALKED OVER.
HUH?
カラオケ
KAREN?
OH, RETSUKO!

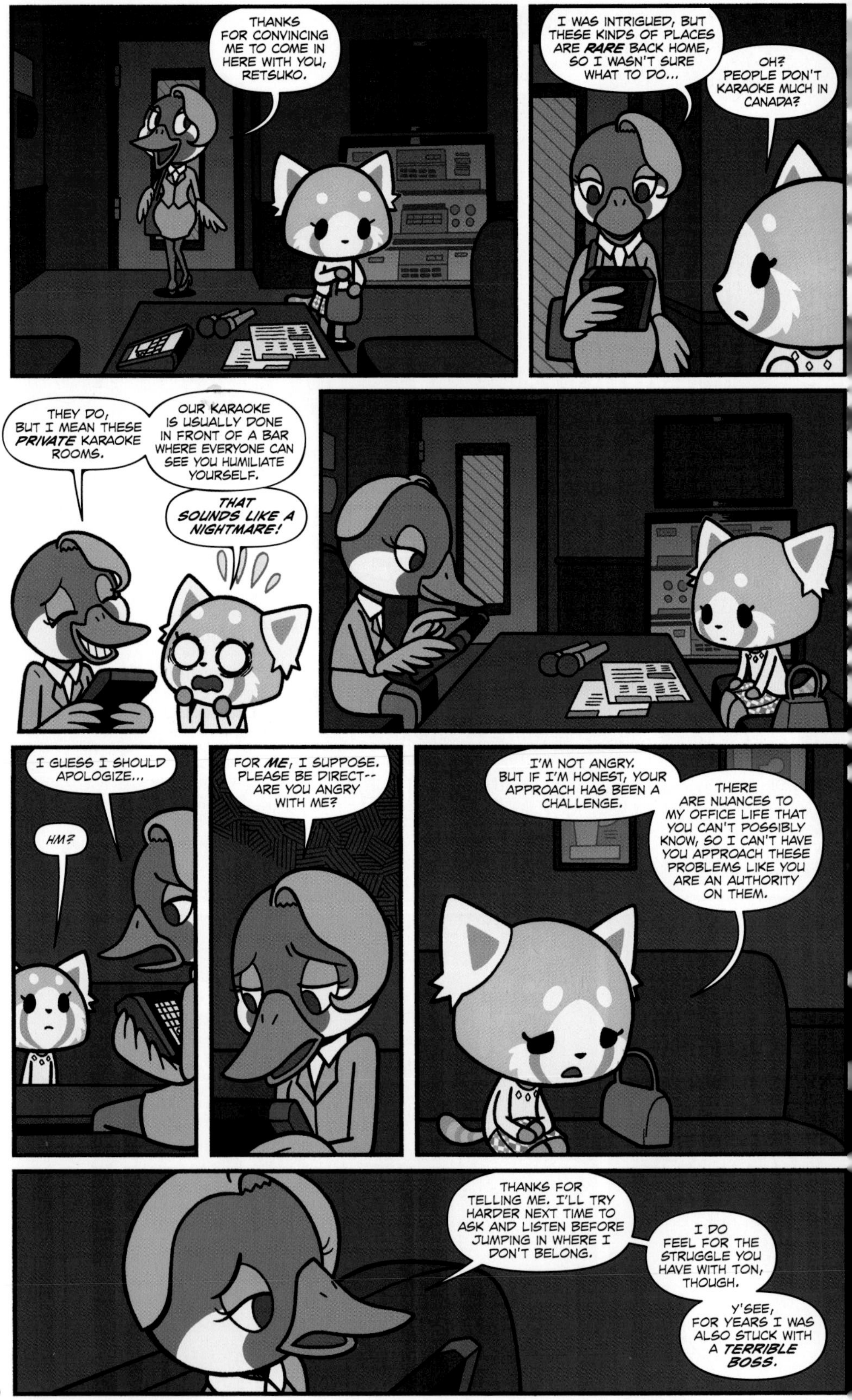
THANKS FOR CONVINCING ME TO COME IN HERE WITH YOU, RETSUKO.
I WAS INTRIGUED, BUT THESE KINDS OF PLACES ARE *RARE* BACK HOME, SO I WASN'T SURE WHAT TO DO...
OH? PEOPLE DON'T KARAOKE MUCH IN CANADA?
THEY DO, BUT I MEAN THESE *PRIVATE* KARAOKE ROOMS.
OUR KARAOKE IS USUALLY DONE IN FRONT OF A BAR WHERE EVERYONE CAN SEE YOU HUMILIATE YOURSELF.
THAT SOUNDS LIKE A NIGHTMARE!
I GUESS I SHOULD APOLOGIZE...
HM?
FOR *ME,* I SUPPOSE. PLEASE BE DIRECT-- ARE YOU ANGRY WITH ME?
I'M NOT ANGRY. BUT IF I'M HONEST, YOUR APPROACH HAS BEEN A CHALLENGE.
THERE ARE NUANCES TO MY OFFICE LIFE THAT YOU CAN'T POSSIBLY KNOW, SO I CAN'T HAVE YOU APPROACH THESE PROBLEMS LIKE YOU ARE AN AUTHORITY ON THEM.
THANKS FOR TELLING ME. I'LL TRY HARDER NEXT TIME TO ASK AND LISTEN BEFORE JUMPING IN WHERE I DON'T BELONG.
I DO FEEL FOR THE STRUGGLE YOU HAVE WITH TON, THOUGH.
Y'SEE, FOR YEARS I WAS ALSO STUCK WITH A *TERRIBLE BOSS.*

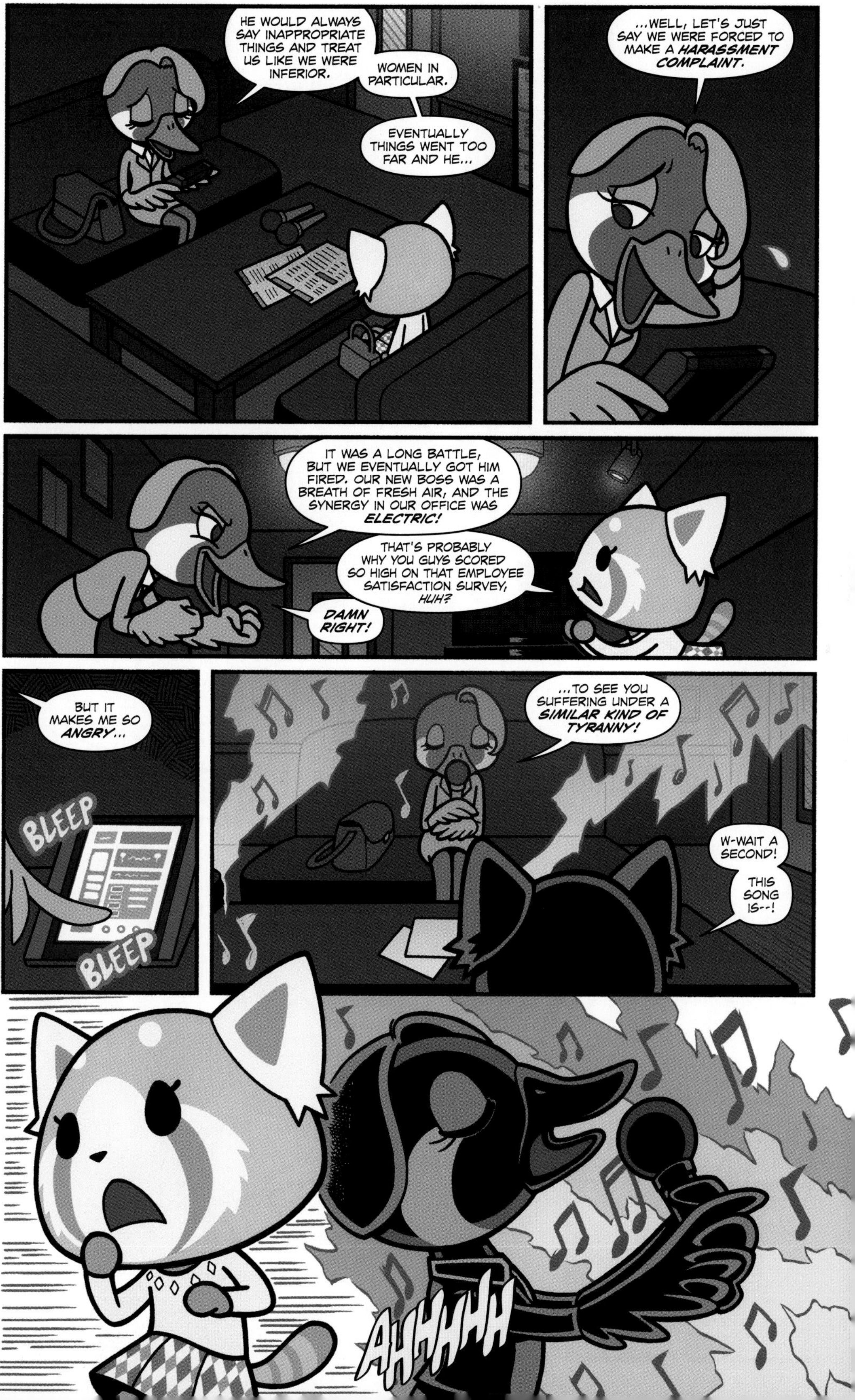
HE WOULD ALWAYS SAY INAPPROPRIATE THINGS AND TREAT US LIKE WE WERE INFERIOR.
WOMEN IN PARTICULAR.
EVENTUALLY THINGS WENT TOO FAR AND HE...
...WELL, LET'S JUST SAY WE WERE FORCED TO MAKE A HARASSMENT COMPLAINT.
IT WAS A LONG BATTLE, BUT WE EVENTUALLY GOT HIM FIRED. OUR NEW BOSS WAS A BREATH OF FRESH AIR, AND THE SYNERGY IN OUR OFFICE WAS ELECTRIC!
THAT'S PROBABLY WHY YOU GUYS SCORED SO HIGH ON THAT EMPLOYEE SATISFACTION SURVEY, HUH?
DAMN RIGHT!
BUT IT MAKES ME SO ANGRY...
BLEEP
BLEEP
...TO SEE YOU SUFFERING UNDER A SIMILAR KIND OF TYRANNY!
W-WAIT A SECOND!
THIS SONG IS--!
AHHHHH

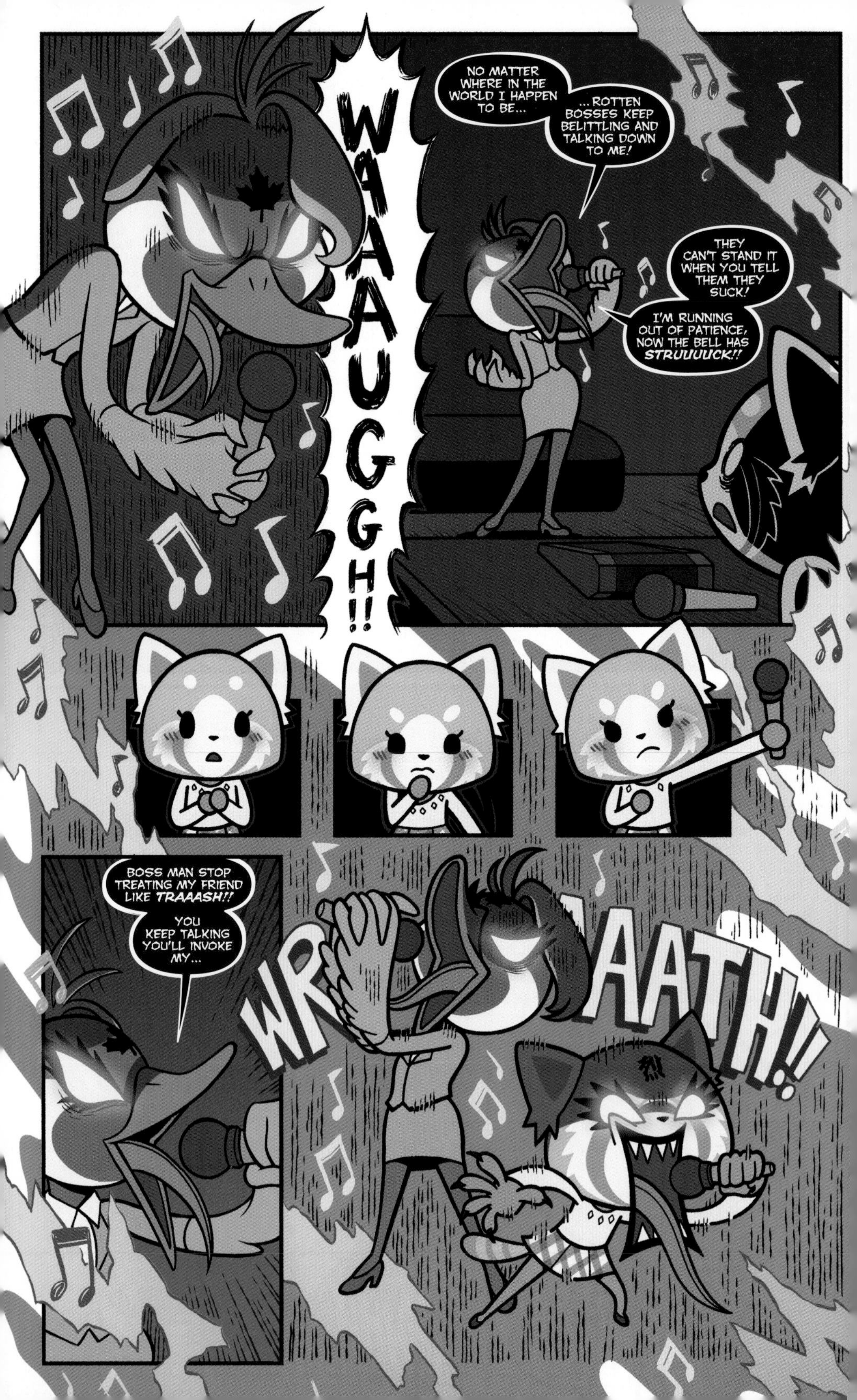
WAAAUGGH!!
NO MATTER WHERE IN THE WORLD I HAPPEN TO BE...
...ROTTEN BOSSES KEEP BELITTLING AND TALKING DOWN TO ME!
THEY CAN'T STAND IT WHEN YOU TELL THEM THEY SUCK!
I'M RUNNING OUT OF PATIENCE, NOW THE BELL HAS STRUUUUCK!!
BOSS MAN STOP TREATING MY FRIEND LIKE TRAAASH!!
YOU KEEP TALKING YOU'LL INVOKE MY...
AATH!!

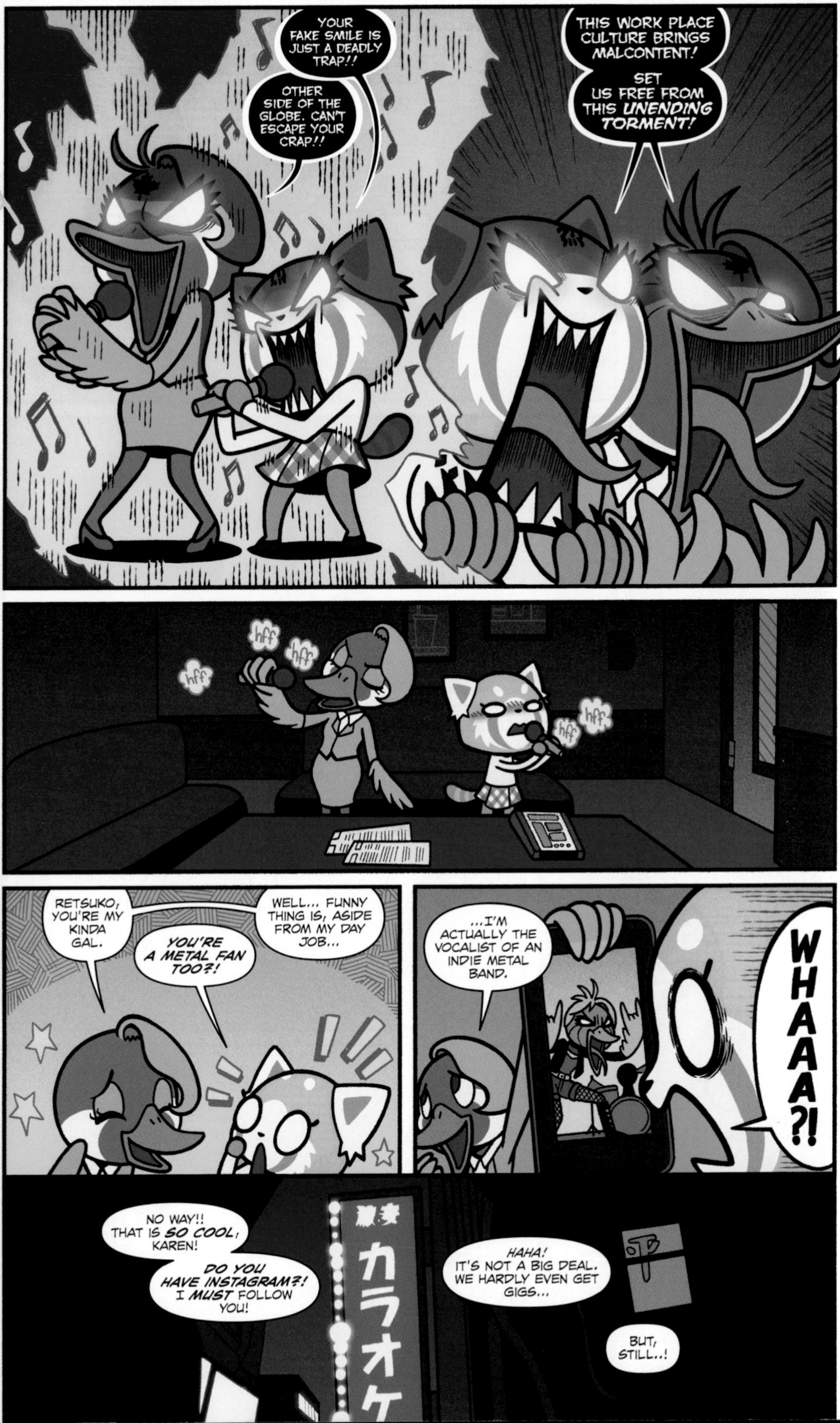

YOUR FAKE SMILE IS JUST A DEADLY TRAP!!
OTHER SIDE OF THE GLOBE. CAN'T ESCAPE YOUR CRAP!!
THIS WORK PLACE CULTURE BRINGS MALCONTENT!
SET US FREE FROM THIS UNENDING TORMENT!
hff
hff
hff
hff
hff
RETSUKO, YOU'RE MY KINDA GAL.
WELL... FUNNY THING IS, ASIDE FROM MY DAY JOB...
YOU'RE A METAL FAN TOO?!
...I'M ACTUALLY THE VOCALIST OF AN INDIE METAL BAND.
WHAAAA?!
NO WAY!! THAT IS SO COOL, KAREN!
DO YOU HAVE INSTAGRAM?! I MUST FOLLOW YOU!
カラオ
HAHA! IT'S NOT A BIG DEAL. WE HARDLY EVEN GET GIGS...
BUT, STILL..!

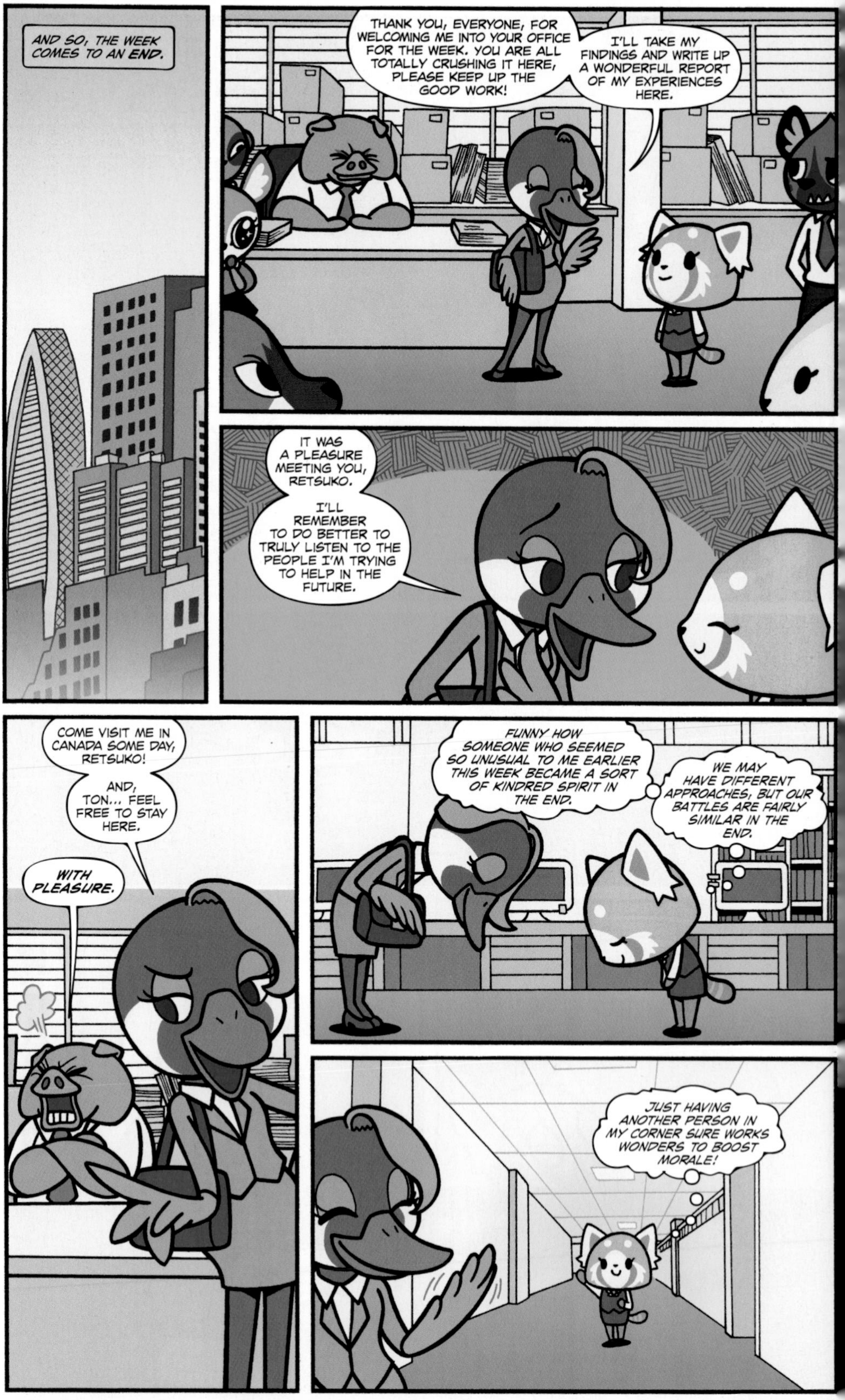
AND SO, THE WEEK COMES TO AN END.
THANK YOU, EVERYONE, FOR WELCOMING ME INTO YOUR OFFICE FOR THE WEEK. YOU ARE ALL TOTALLY CRUSHING IT HERE, PLEASE KEEP UP THE GOOD WORK!
I'LL TAKE MY FINDINGS AND WRITE UP A WONDERFUL REPORT OF MY EXPERIENCES HERE.
IT WAS A PLEASURE MEETING YOU, RETSUKO.
I'LL REMEMBER TO DO BETTER TO TRULY LISTEN TO THE PEOPLE I'M TRYING TO HELP IN THE FUTURE.
COME VISIT ME IN CANADA SOME DAY, RETSUKO!
AND, TON... FEEL FREE TO STAY HERE.
WITH PLEASURE.
FUNNY HOW SOMEONE WHO SEEMED SO UNUSUAL TO ME EARLIER THIS WEEK BECAME A SORT OF KINDRED SPIRIT IN THE END.
WE MAY HAVE DIFFERENT APPROACHES, BUT OUR BATTLES ARE FAIRLY SIMILAR IN THE END.
JUST HAVING ANOTHER PERSON IN MY CORNER SURE WORKS WONDERS TO BOOST MORALE!

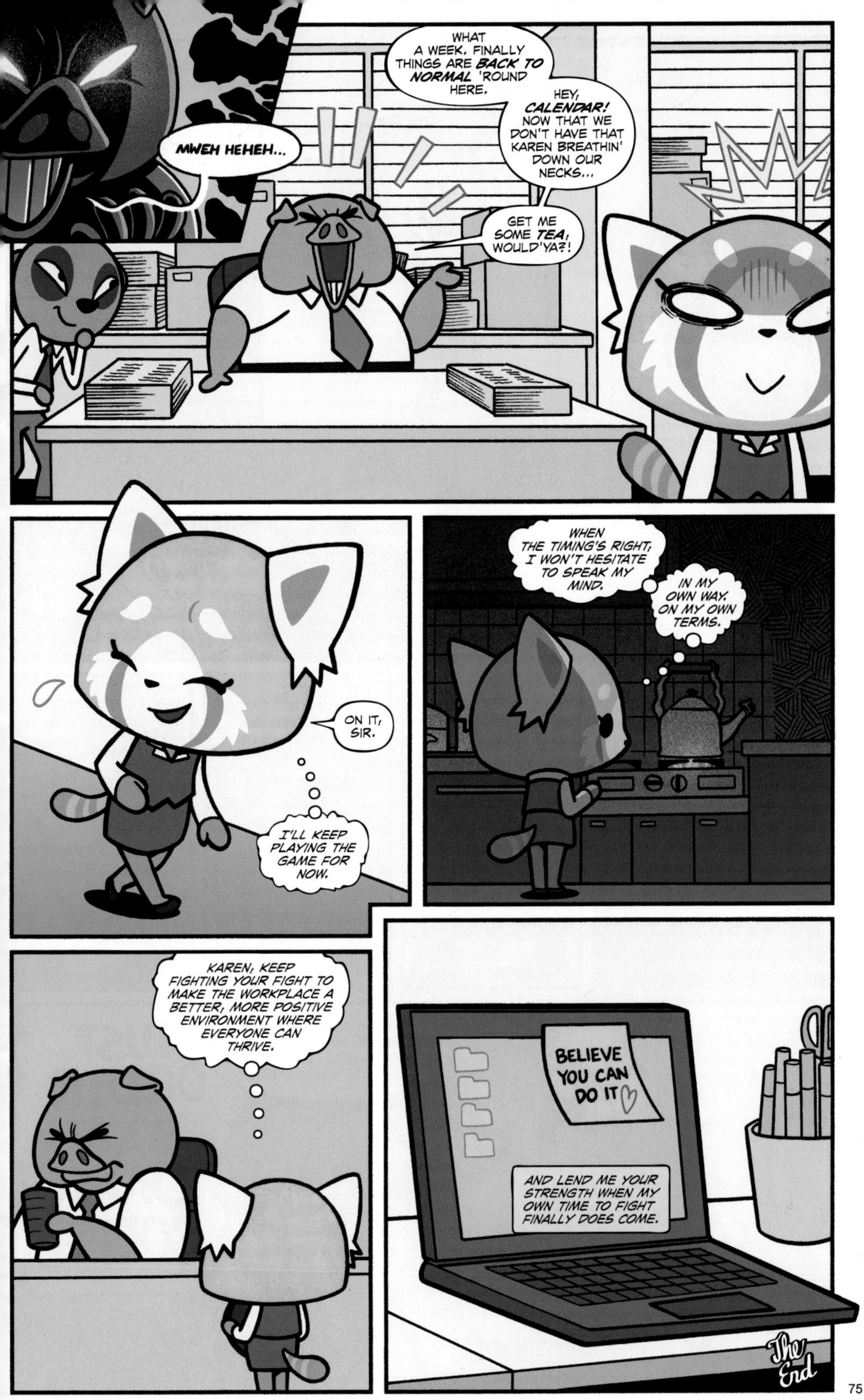
MWEH HEHEH...
WHAT A WEEK. FINALLY THINGS ARE BACK TO NORMAL 'ROUND HERE.
HEY, CALENDAR! NOW THAT WE DON'T HAVE THAT KAREN BREATHIN' DOWN OUR NECKS...
GET ME SOME TEA, WOULD'YA?!
ON IT, SIR.
I'LL KEEP PLAYING THE GAME FOR NOW.
WHEN THE TIMING'S RIGHT, I WON'T HESITATE TO SPEAK MY MIND.
IN MY OWN WAY. ON MY OWN TERMS.
KAREN, KEEP FIGHTING YOUR FIGHT TO MAKE THE WORKPLACE A BETTER, MORE POSITIVE ENVIRONMENT WHERE EVERYONE CAN THRIVE.
BELIEVE YOU CAN DO IT
AND LEND ME YOUR STRENGTH WHEN MY OWN TIME TO FIGHT FINALLY DOES COME.
The End

A METAL MOMENT WITH RETSUKO

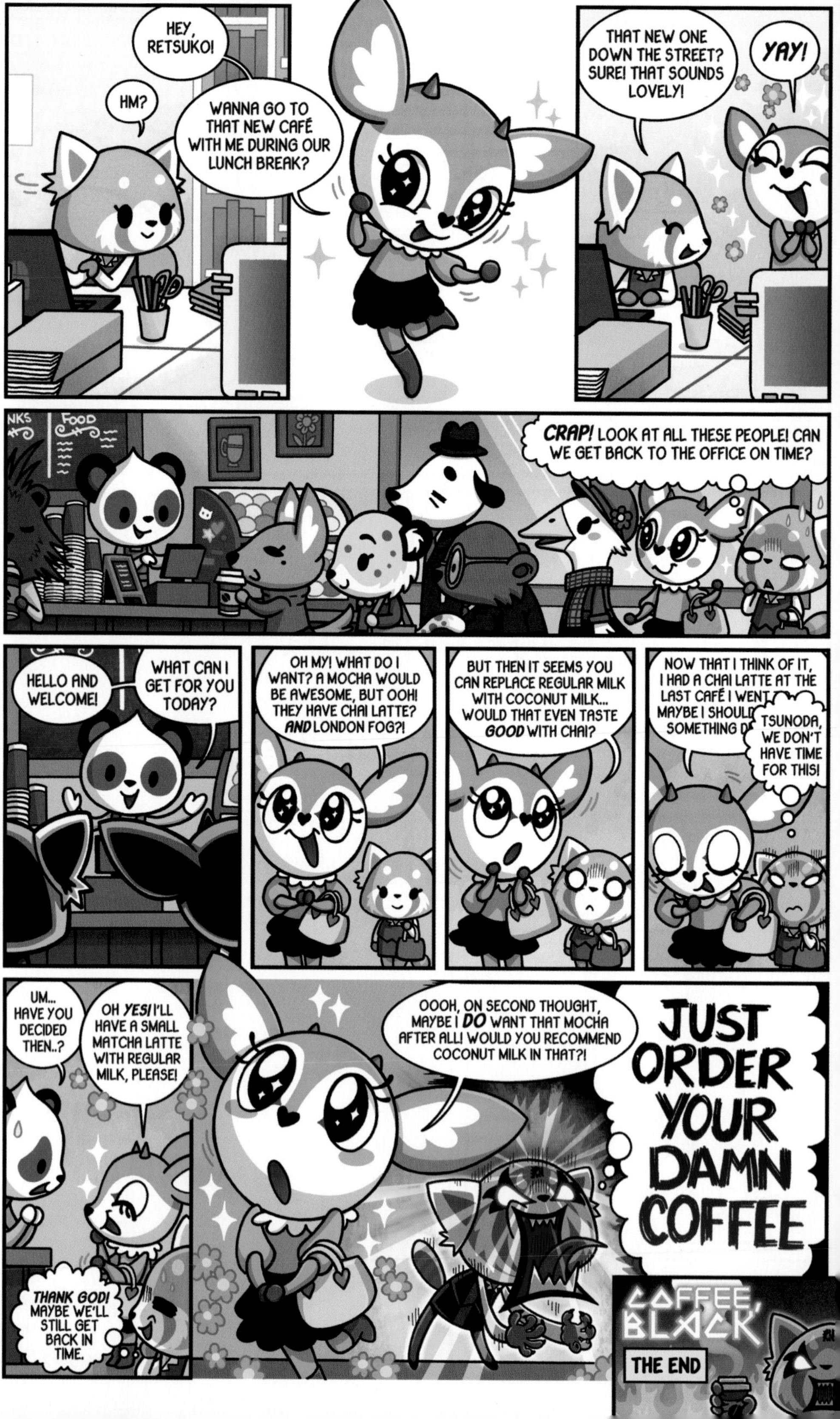

HEY, RETSUKO!
HM?
WANNA GO TO THAT NEW CAFÉ WITH ME DURING OUR LUNCH BREAK?
THAT NEW ONE DOWN THE STREET? SURE! THAT SOUNDS LOVELY!
YAY!
NKS
FOOD
CRAP! LOOK AT ALL THESE PEOPLE! CAN WE GET BACK TO THE OFFICE ON TIME?
HELLO AND WELCOME!
WHAT CAN I GET FOR YOU TODAY?
OH MY! WHAT DO I WANT? A MOCHA WOULD BE AWESOME, BUT OOH! THEY HAVE CHAI LATTE? AND LONDON FOG?!
BUT THEN IT SEEMS YOU CAN REPLACE REGULAR MILK WITH COCONUT MILK... WOULD THAT EVEN TASTE GOOD WITH CHAI?
NOW THAT I THINK OF IT, I HAD A CHAI LATTE AT THE LAST CAFÉ I WENT
MAYBE I SHOULD
SOMETHING
TSUNODA, WE DON'T HAVE TIME FOR THIS!
UM... HAVE YOU DECIDED THEN..?
OH YES! I'LL HAVE A SMALL MATCHA LATTE WITH REGULAR MILK, PLEASE!
OOOH, ON SECOND THOUGHT, MAYBE I DO WANT THAT MOCHA AFTER ALL! WOULD YOU RECOMMEND COCONUT MILK IN THAT?!
JUST ORDER YOUR DAMN COFFEE
THANK GOD! MAYBE WE'LL STILL GET BACK IN TIME.
COFFEE, BLACK
THE END